*[handwritten inscription]* Dear Henry

# A DECADE OF STOCK MARKET TURMOIL
## (2000–2010)

*[handwritten inscription]* with best wishes

*[handwritten signature]*

# A DECADE OF STOCK MARKET TURMOIL (2000–2010)

*And How to Profit From It*

## Robert Skepper

Book Guild Publishing
Sussex, England

First published in Great Britain in 2011 by
The Book Guild Ltd
Pavilion View
19 New Road
Brighton, BN1 1UF

Typesetting in Times by
YHT Ltd, London

Printed in Great Britain by
CPI Group (UK) Ltd, Croydon, CR0 4YY

A catalogue record for this book is available from
The British Library.

ISBN 978 1 84624 687 6

# *Contents*

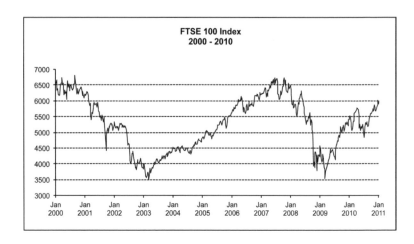

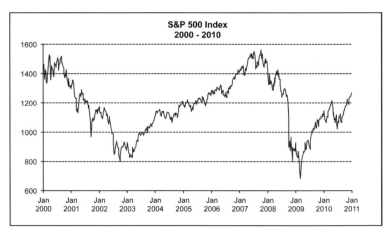

# Introduction

The decade 2000–2010 has arguably been the most turbulent stock market period since trading began in Holland in the seventeenth century. For many equity investors it was the decade from hell. What has made these ten years so fascinating is that they have encompassed, in a historically minuscule time frame, no less than three stock market crashes, plus an implosion of financial markets on a monumental scale.

Such a combination in such a limited time-span is unprecedented. For the student it represents perhaps a hundred years of experience condensed into ten. For the rest of us it poses a number of questions regarding why and how capitalism nearly imploded at a time of relative political stability, during which the world economy was arguably in better shape than ever before.

This should have been a decade of serene and steady economic progress enhanced by major technological advancement; instead it ended in crisis. Having been dealt such an excellent hand, why did we (in the West) so nearly blow it?

In this book I do not attempt to give a direct answer to this, but hope that readers, by revisiting the financial events as they happened (and as recounted in the newsletters that I wrote at the time), can perhaps divine some of the reasons and recognise the fault lines in the regulatory and supervisory systems that precipitated the crisis.

Readers should also be able to perceive that there are permanent principles of investment, which, if adhered to, enable one to come through such difficult and traumatic stock market gyrations unscathed (and even wealthier). Furthermore, over the next ten or twenty years we should be able to benefit from the lessons learnt from these past failures, leading to much more benign conditions for making money in stock markets.

In the early chapters I have also covered the two main political themes that underpin the economics of the UK: the changing relationship between the UK and the EU; and the weakening of the UK economy during Gordon Brown's stewardship.

It is also important in investment always to keep an eye on the wider scene, not least because the media tends to over-dramatise adversity (nobody makes money peddling good news), leading sometimes to exceptional investment opportunities, as irrational fears push prices to bargain levels.

There is no intention to tell people how to invest, or what they should do to be a success at it. Visit the financial section of any bookshop and there are dozens of books claiming to be an infallible guide to stock market success. However, such books are unlikely to make you rich; the secret to successful investing is the intelligent application of well proven business principles, and a reasonable understanding of the unpredictable nature of stock markets themselves. There has been no better period than the last decade to improve that understanding.

Paradoxically, in the stock market – unlike in most walks of life where you learn by experience – all too often investors do quite the opposite, and draw quite the wrong conclusions from their experiences. They simply commit the same mistake in a different asset class! They blame the failure on the asset class rather than their incorrect assessment of the price they paid for it. It matters little what asset class you buy, be it equities, bonds, property, or antiques for that matter; if you overpay, or get sold a fake, you will lose money.

It also helps if you can develop a degree of philosophical detachment from violent short-term swings in sentiment. These will be with us so long as the twin forces of greed and fear embodied in human nature itself do not miraculously change.

But everyone has to work out his or her own investment methodology to suit their temperament, and stick to it. That is why you cannot run an investment portfolio successfully with a committee. If you interfere with the style of the person running the investments you end up with a compromise, like a trifle. Any chef will tell you that a trifle consists of the leftovers from the previous week's desserts camouflaged with custard.

Investment management lends itself particularly poorly to back-seat driving. But that does not mean a fund manager and those to whom he, or she, is accountable should not engage in lively debate. Nobody in our business has a monopoly of wisdom. But having laid down the strategy it is best to leave the tactics to the general appointed for the campaign ahead.

It would be encouraging for investment health generally if more people would manage their own investments as occurs in the USA. What I would describe as the 'professional amateur' can be every bit as successful and not infrequently more so than the 'professional professional'. The more widely that investment decision making is spread, the greater the likelihood that markets will behave more rationally. It is unhealthy that some 70% of UK investment management is currently controlled by a mere 16 large institutions.

I do indicate some of the more obvious traps to avoid. But one is always learning, and there is no quicker place to learn than difficult markets.

Stock markets behave unpredictably. That is their character. At any one time the prices are a mixture of value, discount and sentiment. The manner in which these parameters interact can dramatically affect (by up to a hundred per cent or more) the price of the same asset.

The most important thing is to get the value right in the first place, as this is the one component over which you do have some real control. The other two can be random and illogical, and sometimes for longer than anyone can believe possible; or as John Maynard Keynes put it: 'Markets can be "wrong" for longer than your bank account can hold out.'

Yet my experience of most investors is that they are always more concerned about 'what the market is going to do next' than concentrating on what their investments are going to do next. Trying to outwit markets has proved in general a futile exercise, as those who have recently put their faith in hedge funds have discovered. Six out of ten of the 300 wealthiest UK families stated that in 2009 they held one or more hedge funds, which they could not 'get out of'. This is shorthand for being more or less worthless.

Many hedge funds basically sell themselves on the promise that they will make you money whether markets go up or down – i.e. by outwitting markets. This seems to me one of the most false assurances ever given in the history of financial markets. It appropriately reached its climax in the Madoff scandal, where almost $50 billion was creamed off wealthy investors. They and their advisors were taken in by the claim, fraudulently given as it turned out, that Bernard Madoff could and *was* making ten per cent a year every year irrespective of what financial markets did.

Christopher Fildes, the former financial editor of the *Daily Telegraph,* wrote an amusing article in *The Spectator* in 2005 about hedge funds with the title: '*Where are the owners' yachts?*' It began:

The hurricane season started early in Florida this year. In May a hedge fund blew away leaving some seriously rich people seriously poorer – the two Koreans who managed the fund seem to have left. So it's no good asking them, and the money is unlikely to blow back again. Nothing crooked just bad luck and bad brains met together in an effort to do something that couldn't be done in the first place.

The world has a lot to thank the 1933 US regulators for. They came up with the Glass-Steagall Act of that year. This separated retail deposit-taking banking from investment banking activities. It kept the world's financial system on an even keel for more than 70 years. It was a very simple but highly effective piece of financial legislation. Glass-Steagall was repealed by US President Bill Clinton in 1999, its repeal having been previously turned down twice by President Reagan. Within ten years of its repeal we were back into another banking crisis.

As that excellent stock market historian David Schwartz put it:

The answer appears to be quite clear to me. The Glass-Steagall Act of 1933 forced US banks to divest themselves of risky activities. The country sailed through the rest of the century with no banking crisis. It was repealed in 1999, and hey presto a fresh banking crisis of monumental proportions soon emerged.

It is not surprising that many specialists in international banking, such as leading British economist John Kay, have called for a return to 'narrow banking'; Paul Volcker, arguably the greatest central banker America has produced, has also now called for a formal separation of the risky investment banking activities from retail deposit-taking banks.

After the repeal of Glass-Steagall, investment banks were able to use the massive collateral of their parent retail deposit-taking banks to ratchet up their own risk-taking activities. This was undoubtedly a major contributory factor to the financial meltdown. There were others as well.

# Part 1
# The Background

# 1

## *Who Has Done Best in This Traumatic Decade?*

The economic turmoil of this decade has humbled numbers of allegedly professional fund managers and their clients' money. It has also blown to shreds the concept that there exist so-called foolproof investment management systems, such as 'themes', 'top-down', 'bottom-up' and 'long/short' 'alternatives', 'absolute returns' (usually ending up as absolutely negligible returns), hedge funds and so on. These were, and still are, little more than PR stunts to sell financial products on the back of the fashion *du jour* and to exploit people's fear of what the stock market had previously done to them.

What may surprise the student of investment theory is that the 'Long Only', old-fashioned, vanilla-style investment managers have come through this economic maelstrom relatively unscathed, with most of their client money intact. In the case of the outstanding, such as Warren Buffet, Neil Woodford, Anthony Bolton, Ben Miller, Angus Tulloch and other less high profile names, they have managed to make real money (inflation adjusted gains) in what must be regarded as one of the most difficult stock market periods ever. (In 2010 the FTSE 100 index was still over 1,000 points lower – never mind inflation adjusted – than in 2000.)

I have every confidence that these investors and fund managers will continue to succeed, whatever stock markets throw at them, and the good news for investors today is that all such periods of stock market trauma in the past have, so far, been followed by an era of outperformance.

Significantly none of these outstanding managers have gone in for what has recently become quite a fashionable segment of so-called 'modern portfolio management' under the heading of 'DE-RISKING'.

I believe this is actually a gigantic, and for investors, extremely expensive red herring. It can of course be extraordinarily profitable to financial businesses to trade in so they are keen to promote them. These financial products are often sold under the general heading of 'structured products'. But the problem is that they are sometimes nothing like as de-risked as they look, or are made to look.

The creators of these products design them in order to make themselves money whatever happens. That is the bottom line. Typically in a 'retail- structured product' the hidden charge is likely to be between 4% and 7% of the capital you invest. Also the word 'guarantee' seems to be employed rather generously in the promotion of these products. For example, you are 'guaranteed' say 150% of the upside of the FTSE 100 over five years and you are 'guaranteed' your money back if the FTSE 100 does not fall more than so much. However, you are far from risk free.

The one event you would expect to be covered for – a big fall in the market – is exactly what you are not protected against. What is worse is that if at any point during the tenure of the product the markets fall more than the trigger point after which your money back is no longer guaranteed, then your loss may be double the fall in the market or even more depending on how much extra upside you were offered.

There are also often very stiff penalties, which come into

play if, due to unforeseen circumstances following purchase, you need early withdrawal of your investment.

But the real point is that if you don't want to take a risk then don't invest in whatever it is in the first place. It stands to reason that if you don't want to take the risk, whoever takes it off you is going to want most (if not all) your profit in return. Funds that claim they will protect you from the downside usually end up by 'protecting' you even more vociferously from the upside!

If you really want to reduce your risk against a fall in market prices then you or whoever sells you protection has to buy 'Put' options. Statistically nearly 90% of all options expire 'worthless', but that is generally how protection is bought against market falls. For example, you or the fund has paid a series of premiums to protect you or itself against something that may only happen when so many premiums have been paid that most of the upside has been washed away.

All these top fund managers clearly take the view that long-term returns are diminished, not enhanced by such de-risking activities and the cost of them.

The least expensive way to limit your risk is simply to limit the percentage of your assets you commit to any higher risk asset class.

So what is it that makes these particular managers so unique? I would compare them to the captains of a successful fishing fleet. Firstly, they have to be first-class mariners, which in stock market terms means sound stock pickers.

Then, the captain of such a fleet is faced with perpetual uncertainty. There are times when the sea is as deceptively calm as a millpond, and fish are abundant. Making money seems too easy to be credible. Then out of nowhere a storm blows up. The unwary mariner, or he who has ventured into treacherous waters to get the extra big catch, may lose his entire haul. This has to be jettisoned just to save the ship.

Those that have gone even further afield in a speculative fishing orgy may not make it back to port at all (typically, the over-leveraged).

Then there are times when the seas are violent and furious, and most fishermen stay determinedly in harbour, especially if they have been caught out by a previous storm. Fish becomes scarce and the price soars. You, who have courageously gone out into the storm, but not with all your boats, catch some fish, land your haul as the storm mysteriously abates (as so often they do), then sell your catch for a fortune.

The timid simply stay in port until the sea is once again dead calm. By this time the braver souls have already plundered the most valuable fish, so when the meek finally venture forth there is little of value left for them.

The last decade in stock market terms has had all these phases, and more than once. It has wiped out large numbers of greedy captains and poor mariners; and those too timid to leave port have missed the catches altogether, or set sail just before the next storm has brewed in what had seemed deceptively like calm seas. And after such a decade of stormy seas blowing up out of nowhere, many big investment institutions are still riding at anchor in port in a pool of sovereign debt. Let us hope it does not turn into a quagmire of such.

This alone means it is likely that when these large institutional investors do finally sail out of port to ride the equity waves, equities will still have a long way to go up.

Are there any new lessons to be learnt? According to one of the most successful exponents of British foreign policy, Lord Palmerston, we should have 'no permanent friends, only permanent interests'. I would suggest that when it comes to investing there are no permanent lessons, only the permanent principles, and these are ignored at one's peril.

There are lessons to be learnt from everything in life, but they are seldom obvious, and with stock markets even less so.

That is why people go on making the same mistakes. Stock markets tend to behave like viruses. They mutate in response to what has previously been thrown at them. So what has happened yesterday is unlikely to be much use in pointing to what will occur tomorrow. This may be the fallacy that brings down computer-generated systems of investment. These are based on the assumption that past patterns of behaviour under similar circumstances will always replicate in the future. Most of the time they do, but when they don't, the divergence is likely to be very large, and lethal to the computer system.

What everybody is already excited about, or indeed fearful of (or simply knows about) is seldom possible to make money from. Ben Miller of the Legg Mason fund that outperformed the S&P 500 equities index, 14 years in a row, stated: 'You can't make money out of something that has already happened.'

One of the enduring paradoxes of retail investment is that money is almost always raised from the hapless public at the worst possible time, when the asset class of whatever it is, say a property fund or emerging market fund or commodity fund, has already done well for five years. This is the famous, or notorious, five-year record used by fund promoters to sell their products, and is encouraged by The Regulator.

As another legendary fund manager, James Caulfeild of M&G Investments, stated many years ago to me: 'The trouble is (with our industry) the only time you can raise money is when you shouldn't, and the time when you should, you can't.'

James ran, among other funds, the M&G pension fund, which averaged 17% compound growth for 20 years, leading to a number of happy M&G retirees spending much of their retirement on the beaches of the West Indies.

The process of how you choose investments is much more important than what 'the market' is going to do next or what deduction you can make from past performance. The truest statement made in all market promotions is the one in small print that nobody reads: 'Past performance is no guarantee of future performance.' In fact it would probably be more accurate if it said: 'Past performance is most likely not to be replicated in the future! Too often it is not!'

I believe it is more an issue of the old and permanent principles of finance. These could probably be summarised as follows, though many successful entrepreneurs, businessmen and investors would have their own versions:

1. Never forget that making money always has been and always will be difficult. The stock market is no different from any other medium of business in this respect, though there are times when it appears to look ridiculously easy. These are usually followed by a period when the effortlessly made money disappears even more effortlessly.

2. There is no such thing as a safe investment. That includes cash and government securities. Within 50 years most of these so-called 'safe' investments will have lost 90% of their purchasing power. Yet, in the UK, organisations that control pension funds are being forced to hold ever higher quantities of them by regulators.

    The horizon of a pension fund is 50 years or more. So what is the efficacy of holding something that throughout financial history has lost up to 90% of its value over that time horizon, or certainly since currencies went off the Gold Standard?

    This is what Warren Buffet says about those people who dashed into cash in 2008, when the stock market crashed:

    'Today people who hold cash equivalents feel comfortable. They shouldn't. They have opted for a terrible long-term asset, one that pays virtually nothing and is certain to depreciate in value. Those investors who cling now to cash are betting they can efficiently time their move away from it. In waiting for the comfort of good news they are ignoring Wayne Gretsky's advice: "I try to skate where the puck is going to be, not where it has been".'

All successful investment is a matter of the correct assessment of the risk incurred for the future return achieved; sounds easy, but clearly few people get it right, or else we would all be multimillionaires.

Apart from anything else the stock market abounds with temptations to lead you away from strict objective assessment. When people start asking for a 'tip' you know instinctively you are getting towards the top of whatever it is. But big stock market excitements are highly contagious and incredibly difficult to resist.

We know there is no such thing as a risk free investment. Paradoxically the lowest risks historically have been property and equities, yet regulators deem them the highest risk.

By contrast, the highest risks over the long term have been all currencies and sovereign bonds (most of which have reneged partially or wholly on their face value at some point in time in their history). Yet the regulators deem these the safest.

3. There is no magic formula. Anyone who claims they have got one is a fraud.
4. The simple rule of business is to try to buy cheap and sell dear. This applies to the stock market even more than anywhere else.

Yet almost alone of markets, the stock market by its very nature tempts people to do the opposite.

Resist the strong sucking power of a booming market, just as you must resist the panic inducement of a crashing stock market to sell cheap. As in other walks of life if you buy 'dear' you usually live to regret it.

5. Ignore forecasters. None of them get it right frequently enough to rely on. If you think of banks' predictions of foreign exchange each year for the next year end, no bank gets it right other than randomly, and most get it wrong year after year. There is no industry like the finance industry for the sheer volume of false prophets.

6. Finally, in order to avoid losing lots of money in stock markets – and money that tends to be irrevocably lost – avoid bubbles. These are the real wealth destroyers and in the end wipe out momentum investors. Jimmy Goldsmith famously commented: 'When you see a bandwagon developing it is time to start getting off.'

In a bubble you are in a casino, and the rule in casinos is that if you are on a winning streak take your money progressively off the table so what you are risking gets less and less. And never commit new money to an old bubble. That way, when your winning streak ends, and they always do, you are at least left with the earlier profits rather than leaving the casino completely empty-handed.

If there were a quickfire solution to becoming a successful investor, so many people would adopt it that it would quickly become invalidated. As that old sage of Morgan Stanley, Barton Biggs, said many years ago: 'There is no asset class that large amounts of money will not eventually spoil.'

Of course there are other famous dictums of successful investors such as that of Bernard Baruch. He said: 'Never try and buy at the bottom or sell at the top.'

Another useful one is from Anthony Bolton: 'Try to forget the price you paid for a share otherwise it becomes a big psychological impediment to taking the right investment decision.' To this piece of wisdom could be added what Wellington said was necessary for a good general: 'He must know when to retreat and dare to do so.'

The sagacity of these famous investors can guide one to avoid the most obvious traps; their advice should be well heeded.

# 2

## *The Uneasy Relationship Between Britain and Europe*

I was born in France, and lived and worked there for a French company with a subsidiary in Belgium. So from an early age I had some experience of the French in terms of their working practices and their political outlook; I also gained first-hand experience of working inside the Common Market as it was at the time.

The creation of the Common Market had been a huge success for the original six constituent countries (France, Germany, Italy, Belgium, the Netherlands and Luxembourg), and the growth rates approached 4.5% for many years. Meanwhile the UK scraped along at little over 1%.

Early on, a common agricultural policy (CAP) was set up to ensure that the six were never again short of food. Post-war Germany had suffered grave food deprivation for at least three years, and the Dutch had been reduced to eating tulip bulbs towards the end of the war. By 1980 it had been such a success under the impetus of generous internal prices, and other incentives, that the previously mediaeval farming of most of Europe had been catapulted into the twentieth century with a one-off surge in productivity and output.

It is interesting that a parallel event happened in China in the 1990s when farming there was privatised. That unleashed the first great growth phase of the now soaring Chinese economy.

So successful was the CAP that the EU became awash with excessive agricultural produce, leading to wine lakes, butter mountains, beef foothills and olive oil rivers.

The French, by far the largest agricultural producer in Europe, were loath to reform a system of support that ensured that their, by then, massive surplus production, enjoyed the artificially high internal prices of the EU rather than the much lower world prices. So with the French blocking reform, it dragged on for more than a decade. The European consumer bore the cost, which by then of course included the British.

As the only major net importers of food within the EU, the British were the biggest losers. If the UK had pulled out of the EU at that point and sourced its food more cheaply in world markets, the extra burden on the CAP would probably have forced reform much sooner.

The absurdity of prolonging this policy long past its sell-by date gradually became obvious to most people in Britain, and really set the Euro-sceptic bandwagon rolling. While politicians such as Ted Heath had handed down their tablets of wisdom from on high about the great benefits of membership, it had more or less been taken as read. Now the whole thing came under rather greater scrutiny. This was especially true of the creeping, unelected power of Brussels: the reported waste and extravagance; the perceived corruption of a second European administrative machine; and the extra regulations emanating from the bureaucrats there. There were widely held fears among a growing fraternity of Euro-sceptics about the encroachment on UK civil liberties and on British sovereignty.

Bill Cash, who started the Euro-sceptic movement in Parliament in the early 1980s was for years regarded and

13

treated as a fringe eccentric, but by 2000 his views had become widely held. A large proportion of the population had swung from Euro approval to Euro-scepticism.

A letter by Charles Ellerby from Dartford in Kent, printed in the *Daily Telegraph* in 1997, fairly well summed up the mood from the ever-growing Euro-sceptic movement at the time. 'Sir,' he wrote, 'I am 97 and have considerable experience of modern histories of Germany, France, and Belgium. I can only conclude that any Briton in favour of further involvement in Europe seek medical advice.'

Furthermore by 1997 the British economy was now bearing the fruit of Maggie Thatcher's crack down on the public sector with her insistence on good housekeeping; and with a helping hand from North Sea oil it was bowling along considerably better than most EEC countries. These seemed to be increasingly held back by growing state socialism. As the British were dismantling it, other European nations were putting it up. Britain then overtook France to become the fourth wealthiest country.

London had also become the thriving epicentre of the European financial world. This was one major benefit Britain had certainly gained by its membership of the EU. But on the whole, from the very beginning, the British had fitted uncomfortably into Europe, and, as a nation, are still very divided on quite what their role should be. The British civil service had also done its best to shackle the nation with every European rule or directive, seemingly more so than any other participant country. It seems that the civil service, which had been the master of an empire, could not stomach being the servant of Brussels.

Everything that came out of Brussels seemed to be 'goldplated' by the British civil service, which appeared to have a Faustian pact with the god of bureaucracy to turn every molehill of a new directive into a mountain of red tape that ensnares only the British.

The other nations, bar none, took the pragmatic or 'Italian' route of interpreting Brussels with considerable elasticity – sometimes bordering on the skills of Houdini. A recent letter about weed-killers in an English newspaper encapsulates the difference:

> Mr Simmons is correct that Sodium Chlorate, the weed-killer, has now been banned in the EU. Consequently it is widely available throughout France. (MP, London. 21 Nov, 2010.)

Another example was that for three years after British beef (post the CJD/BSE scare) was declared safe, and the import bans into Europe removed, France continued to refuse entry to British beef.

This is what the British MEP, Mr Robert Sturdy, said about it at the time:

> Sir, British farmers have been dealt yet another bitter blow by the European commission's scandalous decision to withdraw from the European Court of Justice the just demand for a £100,000 a day fine on France for its illegal ban on British beef.
>
> What will our government do to remedy this outrageous decision? Will it take up the case now the Commission has shown itself toothless? The European Commission may be satisfied but I am not. This is yet further evidence that the free market is a complete myth.

Today, barring some extraordinary event, the British appear to be too deeply involved to pull out, but for the country that is the second largest contributor and the only nation that runs a permanent trade deficit with the rest of Europe, the UK's influence has been rather pitiful, arguably dangerous to the national interest.

Referring to the fear, enunciated by the then shadow chancellor George Osborne, that the European Union's badly designed new controls would needlessly undermine London's competitive advantage, business and financial commentator Anthony Hilton wrote (*Evening Standard*, 12 June, 2009):

> Any student of the workings of the European Union knows that each of the big countries has its special national interests and there is no point in seeking to change policy in that area unless that country agrees. Thus there can be no change to the Common Agricultural Policy unless France supports it, and no change in heavy industry in, for example, policy towards utilities or chemicals, unless the Germans are on side. When it comes to financial services, which is the UK's core interest, there is no such natural deference to the wishes and special interests of the UK. This is the ultimate failure of British diplomacy over 30 years, but also of British refusal to properly engage constructively with Europe. It is the price paid for being a permanent member of the awkward squad.

The European ship is now very different from the one that Britain joined in 1973. There are now 27 member nations compared to 6 then, and most of the new entrants are ex state-controlled economies of Eastern Europe. They are unlikely to want to exchange the apparatchiks of the communist era for another set of apparatchiks sitting in Brussels.

After the first French '*Non*' to the Treaty of Lisbon, the Conservative MP and former diplomat, Sir Peter Smithers, wrote to *The Times* as follows:

> Sir, as joint secretary of the Brussels conference of United Europe in 1949, a delegate to the parliamentary

assembly in Strasbourg, a foreign office minister in two UK governments, and finally secretary general to the Council of Europe, I would have welcomed the establishment of a European Federation if it was ever in our reach. But in all the above positions it was clear to me that it was contrary to the politico economic realities. Living at the centre of Europe today I know that there is no European country whose citizens wish to be governed by a European government with all of the consequences...

The European Union is now at a very interesting point, economically and politically. As a consequence of its aggrandisement, the political architecture is having to change.

On the economic front, the sclerosis that seemed to be settling on the EU, largely brought about by too high state sectors in too many member countries, has been shaken by the financial maelstrom of 2008.

The European Union is still a very young experiment in historical terms. It has been through a bad patch, but with the rejuvenating blood of the long oppressed Central and Eastern Europeans now running through its veins, Europe may surprise those who label it as a sunset economy. There is a vast well of talent within the diverse nations of the EU and many ancient and prestigious universities within its frontiers.

The future of the EU may well find its most resonant expression in the words of that gallantly outspoken defender of free markets, Václav Klaus, President of the Czech Republic. On taking up the revolving presidency in 2008, he wrote:

The Czech government will hopefully not push the world and Europe into more regulation, nationalisation, deliberalisation and protectionism. Our historical experience gives us a very strong warning in this respect.

As regards the EU's constitutional stalemate, the Czech government will – hopefully – not lead Europe to an ever closer union, to a Europe of regions (instead of states), to a centralised supranational Europe, to an increasingly controlled and regulated Europe from above. We need to weaken labour, environmental, social, health, and other 'standards' that block rational human activity.

The ever accumulating operational burdens imposed on businesses within the EU, together with higher corporate tax rates, puts us at a competitive disadvantage to Asia, as well as leaving less cash available for reinvestment and dividends. When formulating regulation and taxation of the wealth-producing sector, a return to prioritising a level playing field with our international competitors is long overdue in the Brussels thinking. To imagine, as they seem to, that we live in a closed economic capsule is a recipe for relative economic decline in this highly dynamic and competitive world. However, European ingenuity remains undiminished. The fruits of this are being exploited through the international presence of European companies. The lower tax rates of the newcomers from old Eastern Europe may yet be the catalyst for lower rates throughout. All this could make European investment a lot more attractive than it has been.

# 3

## *The Systemic Damage to the UK Economy During the Blair/Brown Years*

There are frequent passing comments on the subject of this chapter in the newsletters that appear later in this book. Britain's domestic stock market no longer counts for much in world markets – a mere 4% of global capitalisation, if you exclude the purely international stocks quoted in the FTSE 100 (those that have less than 10% of their business in the UK). So for equity investors the performance of the UK economy is a very minor part of their investing universe. That said, what may be a storm in a teacup for the rest of the world, is in reality very uncomfortable for UK citizens.

Failure of the UK economy plays out in a spiral of higher and higher taxes, a depleted health service, inferior education, clogged-up motorways, airport delays, degraded rail services and a general reduction in the quality of life.

If we compare the UK's economic situation at the start of the Blair/Brown years with that of its main continental neighbours, and the situation at the end, it is a worrying tale of relative decline. In every department of public services Britain's relative position has deteriorated. In healthcare the UK is now fourteenth out of 16 leading European nations in

19

terms of cancer therapy provision, overtaken by countries significantly poorer than Britain, such as the Czech Republic. Compared to Sweden, for instance, where 60.3% of men and 61.7% of women survive a cancer diagnosis, in the UK figures range between 40.2% to 48% for men, and 48 to 54.1% for women.

Britain's entire output in terms of motorway construction in the last decade has been one tenth of that of France. In rail transport, the high-speed network in Europe has increased by nearly 4,000 miles during the decade; by comparison, Britain has only managed 60 miles. Education is more difficult to evaluate, but Britain's illiteracy is the highest in Western Europe.

And of course in pure economic figures the UK began the period with the lowest unemployment and lowest debt to GDP ratio of the leading European nations; it also had a primary surplus on the government budget of £30 billion a year. Now Britain has the largest primary budget deficit of any of them, except Greece. Britain has seen a sharp rise in national debt, overtaking Germany (and soon France); and if you count at least some of the 2.5 million people claiming invalidity benefit, then altogether the UK has 6.5 million men and women of working age who are not gainfully employed. Thus its true unemployment figure is now among the highest in Europe.

This has been masked for years by Labour's statistical acrobatics and of course its recruitment of over one million extra people into the public sector.

Many of these jobs will turn out not to have been real jobs at all. David Smith of leading British investment managers, Williams de Broë, found that 860,000 public sector jobs were already established between 1998 and the autumn of 2004; this equated to 45% of the 1.9 million extra jobs the Chancellor and his next-door neighbour boasted about.

Perhaps a good example of the value of the jobs created in the public sector is this one:

## *GARBOLOGY OFFICER £20,370–£23,313*

*Job Description: Are you looking for any opportunity to be involved with an exciting new initiative between archaeology and waste management service? Garbology is the archaeology of rubbish, ancient and modern. You can show children in schools how to explore their heritage through the study of waste...*

This was stated without even a hint of irony.

How is it possible that this deterioration could have occurred in such a short period?

The root cause appears to have been a deliberate, far too rapid and excessive transfer of national resources out of the productive sector and into the non-productive sector. It was like a company tripling the size of its head office while reducing the capacity of its production of goods and services for sale.

In 1996 the public sector accounted for about 37% of GDP. After Brown's innings at the Treasury it had reached 45%. Take, on top of this, the £30 billion windfall from selling the 3G licences, the £5 billion a year snaffled from the pension fund industry (at least £50 billion over 10 years), the one-off £5 billion super tax taken off the utilities in Labour's first budget, and that makes another £85 billion vanishing into the public sector swamp.

Here are some typical headlines of this decade:

**Relentless March of State Spending by Martin Beckford and Robert Willet**
They write: Private Sector Now Makes Up Less Than Half the Economy ... Government spending now accounts for more than half the economy for the first time on record.
(OECD figures show that central and local government

spending made up 52.1% of Britain's GDP last year (up from 40% in 1997).

George Trefgarne wrote in the *Daily Telegraph*, 31st January 2005:

**Patricia Hewitt's Pot Plants are a Symbol of Labour's Attitude to Your Money**
It's not quite as bad as Elton John's great penchant for flowers, but Patricia Hewitt's love of pot plants certainly takes some beating – this morning as the trade secretary peers through the foliage she had better reflect on the political consequences of the revelation unearthed in a parliamentary question that she had spent more than £120,000 on pot plants since 2001 – is it just that the DTI's verdant windowsills are emblematic of how casual Labour has been with public money?

**How Many Inspectors Does it Take to Check on How Well a Hospital is Working? Try 102 (and Counting)**
More than one hundred organisations, according to *The Times*, 9th October, 2004, have powers to inspect hospitals, leaving health workers swamped with duplicate demands for information and sapping precious NHS resources.

Richard Tyler, *Enterprise* editor, wrote:

**Red Tape Costs Have Risen £10 Billion Since 1998**
The cost of regulations introduced by Labour since 1998 have risen £10bn to £88bn.

Philip Johnston and Malcolm Moore wrote in the *Daily Telegraph*:

THE SYSTEMIC DAMAGE TO THE UK ECONOMY

## Tick Here to Make Wealth Vanish
## £81 Billion Wasted Each Year
Government waste and useless expenditure is costing
taxpayers £81bn a year – equivalent to £3300 per family
– according to The TaxPayers' Alliance.

## Public Job Drive Raises Workforce to New High
Between March 2002 and March 2003 125,000 jobs were
lost in manufacturing; however, during the same period
137,000 jobs were created in public administration,
education, and health industries. (14 August, 2003)

## Found the Hole They're Pouring Money Into
This article quotes how the Qualifications and Curricu-
lum Authority, established in 1998 with a budget of £10
million, now spends almost £60 million. It goes on to
state that the Cabinet Office says there are 1,000 quan-
gos but the Public Administration Select Committee
claims there are now 9,000.

Eamonn Butler (head of The Adam Smith Institute) in the
*Daily Telegraph* comment and features, 25th June 2009,
wrote:

## That'll be £2.2 Trillion Please
Today is the cost of government day. Average taxpayers
in Britain now have to work almost half a year – 176
days – to pay their share of the cost of running Gordon
Brown's state leviathan.

Bill Jamieson wrote in *The Business*:

## Boomtime in Welfare as Brown's Billions Flood into the Public Sector
Last week's public sector jobs supplement ran to 106

pages in *The Guardian*. Britain, once a nation of engineers, small firms, and shopkeepers is turning into one vast welfare dispensary. If you are not self-administering, chances are you are administered to. A casual look through the bulging jobs section reveals a burgeoning range of care careers:

Vacancies for 'area co-ordination team leaders', 'review and resource enhancement consultants', 'food and health advisors', 'community engagement officers', 'systemic family therapists', 'workplace health counsellors', 'arrest referral drug workers', 'waste policy officers', 'equality and diversity policy managers', 'housing benefit counter fraud managers', 'strategic partnership co-ordinators', 'co-ordination development officers' and 'policy and development managers'. Would anyone notice if every one of these jobs vanished overnight?

*The Guardian* pages bear out the famous dictum of Milton Friedman:

The more money hurled at social and welfare problems the more money ends up in the pockets of social and welfare workers.

Phillip Oppenheim was Exchequer Secretary to the Treasury from 1996 to 1997. The following extract from his letter, published in *The Times* in 2005, encapsulates the wrong turning Labour took for the economy:

From 1979 to 1997 tax fell substantially as a proportion of GDP helping the economy and productivity to grow faster than our main competitors (even manufacturing grew significantly) financing substantial rises in public expenditure.

Since 1997 the tax take has gone up, productivity increases have fallen below those of comparable countries, our much vaunted economic growth has been created by public sector expenditure and private consumption, rather than productive investment. The Labour govt has presided over 8 years of virtually zero growth in manufacturing.

The choice is not lower taxes or higher spending. It's tax too much and you will end up with less to spend.

The reality of this decade is that there has been huge 'non job' creation in the public sector, and expansion of non-productive state activities, much of this under the trumped-up guise of equality, fairness, and health and safety. The rapid elimination of this large, unproductive dead weight on the economy could lead to a much faster turnaround in the UK's economic prospects. It will require stiff political will-power to remove the privileges of waste from their beneficiaries.

# 4

## *The Regulator*

It is not possible to comment on a decade of financial markets without looking at the influence of the role of the local regulator, in the case of the UK, the Financial Services Authority (FSA). It is no mean task to be a good regulator, but there is every reason why the industry should accept nothing less than the highest quality in this regard.

Admittedly, the FSA, since 2001, has only been one third responsible (together with the Treasury and the Bank of England) for banking regulation and supervision. Yet, here I am predominantly concerned with its exclusive role as regulator and supervisor of Britain's investment management industry.

Since the FSA took over in 2001, it has made a very significant impact in safeguarding the retail investor from the mis-selling of financial products and services, through its KYC (Know Your Client) and TCF (Treat Clients Fairly) programmes.

It has also put in place reliable compensation should it happen. Never has the retail investor, who is deemed to know little and is therefore vulnerable to financial exploitation, been better protected, and offered a higher standard of professional engagement. They certainly have the FSA to thank for that.

The FSA has also significantly raised the bar in terms of initial professional training and qualifications before anyone can be licensed to give financial advice; likewise it has put in place mandatory ongoing improvement training. Thus retail investors should be assured a higher quality service in the future.

This is no mean achievement, no doubt as a result of a great deal of hard and dedicated work. Albeit this has been achieved in the short term with a somewhat excessive overlay of costly bureaucracy. The FSA handbook is somewhat of a misnomer as it would require a giant's hand to hold the 16 source books. These run to over 4 million words of rules, guidelines and regulations, which if stacked up would stand over three feet high!

The FSA's task has not been made simpler by also having to incorporate the European MiFID (Markets in Financial Instruments Directive), devised for the whole EU in Brussels, with its additional range of requirements in the regulatory system.

It is to be hoped, however, that over time common sense and the bedding down of the new regulatory framework will lead to some of the more obvious and unnecessarily costly bureaucratic demands on the industry being eliminated.

This letter from *The Daily Telegraph* neatly encapsulates the industry's concern with its soaring charges and mindless bureaucratic overlay:

Headed 'FSA Confetti':

Sir,

The disbanding of the F.S.A. appears to have caused a flurry of activity. Instead of winding down, it appears to be gearing up.

Currently to ensure that companies are 'treating their clients fairly' which any company would do if it wished to remain in business, accounts have to be submitted six monthly. Then there is the GABRIEL (gathering better regulatory information electronically) six monthly reporting to be completed online too.

I have also been given a date to be interviewed by telephone for one and a half hours and have been sent a sixth survey of the FSA's regulatory performance to complete (16 pages). My annual fee demand has now arrived. It has risen by 300% in a recession.

Are they trying to wind me up too?

Eileen Hall, Colgrave, Northants.


However, in the wider area of risk control and assessment, an approach seems to have been taken that is not fully in the interests of the long-term health and effectiveness of the financial industry, and of the savers and investors it is meant to serve.

The prime and overriding purpose of investment is surely: 'The efficient allocation of capital.' The more efficiently it is allocated, the greater wealth creation for everybody, in particular the savers, who supply the capital. That objective should be always uppermost in the minds of any regulator when formulating policy.

At worst, excessive capital flights from one fashion to the next, which seems to have been the hallmark of this decade, can lead to the sort of disaster we have recently undergone.

The regulatory framework in the UK in this decade seems to have addressed this issue largely from the narrow angle of avoiding the repetition of the Equitable Life debacle. They have also assumed under the section of the Act empowering them to supervise 'market stability' that it includes the power to influence, even direct, the decision-making of professional investment managers in the exercise of their asset allocation decisions.

It is more than dubious that The Act intended such powers for the FSA under the guise of assuring market stability.

The result has been directives that have encouraged conformity, and benchmark shadowing, leading to short-termism and inappropriately imposed risk assessments. This actually exacerbates herd-like movements. As Maynard Keynes once observed:

> It is the long term investor, he who most promotes the public interest, who will in practice come in for the most criticism, wherever investment funds are managed by committees or boards or banks. For it is the essence of his behaviour that he should be eccentric, unconventional, and rash in the eyes of average opinion. If he is successful that will only confirm the general belief in his rashness, and if in the short run he is unsuccessful, which is very likely, he will not receive much mercy.

The regulator should try to create a framework where such persons are understood, not vilified, where robust differences of opinion are encouraged, not stifled, and where independent thinking is not compromised by fear of regulatory reprisal.

Benchmarking is the abdication of any attempt to allocate capital at all. Imposing standard benchmarks for all is the start of command-style interference – 'the men in Whitehall (or the Kremlin) know best.'

Benchmarks should never be the subjective opinion of the few, however elite, who think they know better than the market. Individual investment management companies, be they life companies, retail fund managers, boards of trustees of pension funds or private trusts, should formulate their own asset allocation benchmarks.

Diversity of opinion is at the very heart of stable and rational financial markets. It is when everybody thinks the same, or is made to think the same, that they risk becoming unbalanced, and even wildly irrational.

It is quite perverse that the APCIMS (Association of Private Client Investment Managers and Stockbrokers) should lay down a single risk benchmark for all its member firms, which appears to update insufficiently, regardless of significant economic changes or evolution in the wider world. Each member firm should devise its own asset allocation benchmarks, and adjust them as it sees fit, according to circumstances, as they change.

The current standard risk profile, apparently set in cement, automatically puts cash and government bonds as the lowest risk, and equities as the highest risk. This is, or can be, in certain economic circumstances, nonsense. The relative risk of different financial assets is changing all the time as the prices of these products change relative to each other. Therefore the relative risk assessments should alter too.

To keep to the same benchmark regardless of change of background economic circumstance is about as stupid as trying to ram a square peg into a hole that is now round but started off square.

It should be left to the professionals in capital markets to determine their own benchmarks of risk, as the aggregate of these different independent opinions is likely to be better. The regulator is there to see that such decisions are carried out with integrity, and that markets are not being deliberately manipulated by dissemination of false information or otherwise. But they should no more lay down what constitutes the correct risk profile than the Department of Industry should tell Rolls-Royce how to make its aero engines.

It appears that our regulator, far from putting these key issues at the very heart of its agenda, has not really been thinking along these lines.

As it happens, a substantial part of the fund management

industry in London consists of the production of investment products for international investors to choose from on their merits. These fund managers are completely free to exercise their own professional judgement within the remit of what their fund aims to do. They may measure the performance of their funds against the indices of whatever this aim is. But those that shadow the indices face the very real accusation that they are charging an active management fee for not managing.

The competition of free markets will ensure the promotion of the best and the weeding out of underperformers. Consequently there are many fine fund management groups spread over the UK offering a strong range of investment products from which the world of investors can choose.

The problem is that UK retail funds managers, insurance companies and pension fund trustees do currently face significant regulatory constraint in the free exercise of their judgement as to what proportions of their capital they may allocate across different asset classes.

# Part 2
# The Newsletters

This next section provides a selection from a series of monthly newsletters I wrote between 1998 and 2010. I have endeavoured to extract only the most relevant parts and I have chosen a maximum of six from any one year, except 2009. Our industry is rather prone to waffle and hopefully some of this has been culled.

I have started with extracts from 1998 to 1999 because they demonstrate how the fund management industry was not coping with the changes going on in the business world as a result of the development of the Internet. This led to a wide scale spurning of the IT sector just as the new technology took off, causing serious underperformance against the indices. So they then decided *en masse* to shadow the benchmarks, which they could not beat, and plunge into the IT sector as well. That helped to cause the great Tech bubble.

# 5

## *1999*

### Market and Currency Update – 1 October

There is no technological advance that has so divided the generations as the arrival of the Internet. In the UK there are now believed to be 10 million users and according to a survey 57% are under the age of 34. Probably the remaining 43% are between the age of 34 and 40.

In a recent survey of British industrial leaders over 60% said they found the Internet 'a turn-off'. This is presumably because most of British industry is led by the over fifties. [*The interesting contrast of attitude here with America was that many of the elderly in the USA were taking to the Internet as if it was a new elixir of life, while in the UK the over fifties didn't seem to want to know.*]

The credibility gap is very evident in the stock market. Internet stocks are not valued at 100 x earnings but 100 x sales and they are largely bought up and invested in by the younger generation, while all the wise old heads shake in disbelief. Actually it is rather difficult to know where the wisdom lies – with the young who see the future potential; or the old who don't understand the future and assume, whatever it is, that it is thoroughly over-valued?

That the Internet will change the way the retail economy

operates is perhaps one of the most obvious results of the new technology. Already on average the aggregate price of all goods sold over the Internet in the US is 13% cheaper than the retail alternative through traditional outlets, and this in spite of the extra cost of delivery.

So far the dissemination of information seems to be the single biggest benefit of the Internet, with scientific and medical information becoming available much more quickly to all those who need it, leading to faster research and more rapid scientific or medical advance. At the moment the Internet's single biggest usage is as an information resource.

As far as investing in the Internet is concerned, the end user's shares are probably much the most speculative, because the technology is in such a very early state of development, and nobody yet knows which areas will succeed and which will fall by the wayside. Meanwhile virtually all end user companies coming to the market are valued on the basis that they are bound to be a success.

A more predictable area for investment is access provision, search engines and producers of the hardware to make all this work, plus the telecom companies who make money out of the use of the system. The growth is assured for them. It doesn't matter who the end users turn out to be so long as the whole operation is growing at some phenomenal rate for a significant number of years, which looks to be the one near certainty of the whole new technology.

But of course these companies, like AOL, Yahoo, Cisco and Sun Microsystems; and then the telecoms beneficiaries, such as Energis and Colt Telecom, are already valued at phenomenal multiples. GEC, now called Marconi, had to pay six x sales for the switch company it purchased in the USA. So there is no cheap way of buying into Internet stocks. One suspects that, as so often happens with all new technologies, future expectation in the stock market wildly exceeds final reality.

When semiconductors first appeared in the early 1960s, the new invention was going to change the world. Texas Instruments, one of the largest companies involved, rose from an IPO price of $5 to $250 by the end of 1962. When the fall-out ensued later on, the price fell to $25, and did not get back to the old peak until 1987.

In 1996 Alan Greenspan, Chairman of the Federal Reserve of the United States from 1987 to 2006, said that Wall Street (then with the Dow Jones index standing at 6,000) was suffering from 'irrational exuberance'. Analysts today, by contrast, believe that the earnings of the S&P 500 index could grow at 16.5% per annum for the next five years, on which basis they state that the market could be 15% undervalued. On the other hand, the Federal Reserve economists point out that only in two years between 1979 and 1997 have earnings actually beaten the forecast. The key economic indicators look too strong for comfort with a growth of 4.1% in 1999, unemployment at a 30-year low at 4.5%, and wage growth rising at 4%.

The Dow Jones is currently trading on a PE of 40 x compared to its historic level of 17 x. Of the top 50 stocks that have driven the US market to its all-time high, 25 have yet to make a profit; therefore, talking in terms of PE is not particularly relevant, but it still gives a hairy feeling to the market.

[*The dot-com frenzy is beginning to gather pace and what was a trickle of investors into Tech is now already a fast flowing river. I saw my job at the time as trying to keep people's feet at least somewhere near the ground.*]

## Market and Currency Update – 1 November
FTSE 100 – 6,284

Marks & Spencer is history. So a lot of young friends have been telling me in recent months. I tempered this by suggesting it was at least 'geography' since it owned its sites unlike most of the other high street chains.

I would agree with them to the extent that it is difficult to see Marks & Spencer reviving under the present board and chief executive. They believe that all they have to do is to reinvent the fashion equivalent of the traction engine. The company would probably stand a better chance if the board room were filled with people like Janet Street Porter, Chris Evans and one of the Spice Girls. They probably wouldn't regard the present board as 'history'; more likely, 'archaeology'. This is the problem with the Internet: it has fossilised the over fifties.

Free markets nevertheless have an uncanny way of sorting out their problems if they are allowed to do so without government intervention. Though at the moment e-commerce on the Internet represents a trifling 0.2% of retail sales in Europe, a mere $5.6 billion, it is expected to multiply to a $112 billion (more than 20 times) in the next two years. Meanwhile in the USA e-commerce is already being used by 21 million people, and is expected to rise to 60 million by 2002 (a quarter of the entire population). But, more significantly, the spend per person is expected to rise from $1,706 a year in 1998 to $6,738 by 2002, implying an increase in value of Internet sales from the current $37 billion (approximately) per annum to $407 billion in 2002.

The big worry for everybody with bricks and mortar overheads is that already products sold over the Internet are averaging 13% cheaper than what is available in the shops. As such, the high street is not only faced with an entirely new medium of competition but, rather worse, the depressing pressure on margins that is likely to permanently devalue the economic worth of its turnover.

Investors in the UK have been concentrating on the dangers to margins from Walmart's arrival on British shores. But it is a bricks and mortar operation. The greater risk is more likely from Amazon's arrival with its multi-billion-dollar arsenal. At some point the sector will become heavily oversold, but it is doubtful whether this point has yet been reached in view of the continuing likely flow of disappointing news.

## Market and Currency Update – 15 December
FTSE 100 – 6,702

*The IT frenzy*

November has been an unforgettable month for IT shares with the biggest monthly rise on record, as investors, both private and institutional, have plunged heedless of valuation into anything that moves. Meanwhile institutions, which have been woefully short of IT stocks in the past, too frightened to buy them because of their volatility, have definitely been carrying out some aggressive window-dressing for the year end, pushing up sharply the prices of the big stocks like Misys, Sage, Logica, Admiral, Sema, etc.

To end the year without reasonable IT representation in their institutional portfolios at a time when IT has literally been the only sector of the market to boom might invite 'a spell of unscheduled gardening' for the fund managers concerned.

Values in the big stocks are now becoming very 'heady'. Equally, once the fund manager window-dressing is over the stocks may sag in the New Year. Small investors are not interested in these stocks. The smaller stocks have been almost entirely propelled by private investors.

Winterflood Securities, the largest market maker in the smaller company universe, describes November thus:

> I have never seen anything like it, the volumes going through the market are huge. The market is euphoric; that's the only word for it ... A lot of people are playing about in a new game without really understanding it.

As for Internet stocks, they are valueless in the sense that they have no assets, and nobody knows how to quantify their potential. They could be likened to a flotilla of Christopher Columbus's ships, all heading west into the unknown, unsure whether they will fall off the edge of the earth or arrive in El Dorado. What is certain is that almost without exception Internet stocks are valued on the assumption of the latter rather than the former. No one flies so high as he who knows not where he is going.

By contrast, in 1986, when Microsoft was launched, it had a flotation value of below $700 million. If investors at the time had known it would be worth around $500 billion 12 years later they would at the time have given it a higher value. Currently they are giving Internet stocks values based on a presumption that they will all do in the next 12 years what Microsoft achieved. For example, Yahoo at $74 billion, Amazon at $30 billion, AOL at $180 billion and Lucent Technologies at $250 billion.

The earnings to support these valuations are at least eight years away. Any hint that the earnings progression is not going to plan at any time during this long period will lead to savage price corrections.

But the Internet is turning the conventional world of business and values upside down, which is making it very difficult for investors to get a dependable 'fix' on what they should hold and which shares in the existing firmament will become 'history'.

This is no time to lose faith in sound companies that have got good dividend yields and have simply been ignored by the market. As Anatole Koleski puts it:

> Supposedly canny Scottish actuaries and London investment managers – having paid dearly for their lack of imagination (in not seeing the opportunities in IT stocks sooner) – are now throwing caution to the winds and joining on the high tech bandwagon with hundreds of billions of pounds, euros and trillions of yen.

## The euro

The performance of the euro has brought a smile to every Euro-sceptic face well ahead of Christmas. We were being lectured for years about the danger of not going into the euro, with dour warnings about the collapsed City of London and the risk of the entire British economy being kicked into the sidelines. Quite the reverse has happened. The City of London is just completing the best year by far in its history, having conducted virtually every major inter-European deal, in many cases where no UK company was even involved.

Today, the 'incorruptible' (I am using the Italian version) Mr Prody warned Britain to make up its mind on the euro and its future role in Europe or 'pay the price of exclusion'. Perhaps what he meant to say but could not was: 'or continue to reap the advantage of exclusion'.

This, however, does not fit at all well with the prime minister's plans, which seem to include being crowned as President of Europe at some future date – a sort of 'spin' – created Napoleon with Peter Mandelson as his Talleyrand.

(Napoleon's description of Talleyrand as 'a shit in a silk stocking' could fit the bill.)

# 6

## *2000*

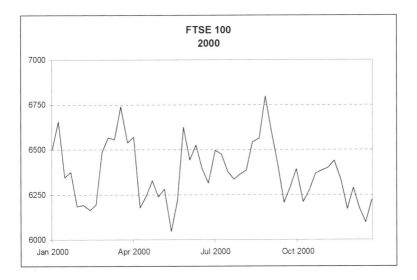

**Figure 1**

## Market and Currency Update – 1 February

*Overview of Davos International Economic Forum*

I spent last week in Davos overviewing the celebrated forum,
which appears even more than last year to have delivered

43

from its mountain of economic talent a yet smaller mouse of content.

The tradition of unblemished prediction of future trends looks safe in their hands. Last year they solemnly predicted it would be the year of the euro. The then new currency would sweep all existing currencies before it as central bankers and corporate treasurers around the world rushed to 'reposition' their reserve weightings by buying the euro.

What happened is that the euro steadily slid downhill.

This year the new message is that nearly everyone will be losing money on the 'It's-all-over-now.com companies'. [*This was a case of crying wolf so many times that when the wolf really did appear, nobody paid any attention.*]

The laws of gravity (it propounded solemnly) are catching up with the Internet and Wall Street. The pure online company is being exposed as a myth. Of the 300 Internet companies floated on the stock market since 1995, it is predicted that roughly 90% will end up worthless. This is reminiscent of the history of US car manufacturing: in the heady days of the 1910s and 20s this industry could boast up to a thousand such companies; yet of these only three now remain. Similarly, of the 2,000 airlines founded between 1930 and 1940 not a single one is around today.

Meanwhile, away from this economic Disneyland, the bourses continued, in spite of such lofty warnings from on high, to dump the shares of traditional businesses and pile ever deeper into the dot-coms.

The FTSE 100 has plunged 600 points since Christmas, as traditional market leaders such as Shell, BP Unilever, Whitbread, Bass, all the utilities and power companies, tobacco companies and banks – indeed practically anything that earns real money – have been sold off. Meanwhile, Sage (now at 130 x historic earnings), ARM and Autonomy (at infinity x historic earnings) have hit new highs. And the trend is not confined to the UK. In Europe Nokia (120 x historic),

Ericsson (90 x), Telefónica and SAP were all at new highs along with Sony and Softbank in Japan. Is this a case of whom the gods wish to destroy they first make mad?

*[By March 2000 the dot-com craze had really gone ballistic and prices were reaching levels that not even a future economic miracle could justify. Just a tiny handful of fund managers kept their heads. Luckily I had sold mostly everything in the tech sector for my clients six months earlier – at prices that looked fantastic at the time but had by now, March, often doubled again. It was largely a matter of experience. I could well remember the last tech boom when the semiconductor was invented. This reduced the size of a computer from a room to a desktop. The companies at the forefront of that new red-hot technology, like Texas Instruments, Fairchild Camera And Instrument Corporation, and Edwin Land's Polaroid Corporation (the equivalent of Cisco, Baltimore Technolgies and JDS Uniphase Corporation of this current tech boom), had soared to 200 x earnings. I had just started at Buckmaster and Moore – a fine company run by a brilliant tyrant, Ian Macpherson. I worked as one of his junior assistants, and you either learnt at double speed or learnt where the exit door was.*

*He wasn't taken in, but us young bucks wanted to have a few and no objection was raised, provided it was our own money. He no doubt reckoned it would be a valuable lesson and indeed it was. Polaroid, at that time valued at $200, and Texas Instruments, at $250, were respectively $25 and $40 a year later.*

*Very sadly, when Wall Street did crash that autumn, eight young men jumped out of windows. That was not a lesson to forget.*

*In March 2000, 80% of all PEP plans (now ISAs) went into tech funds. Poor misguided public: only six months later their money had halved and three years later 90% of it had gone. But that was what the so-called professional fund managers of the*

45

*big institutions selling PEPs had advertised as the best investment.*]

## Market and Currency Update – 1 March
FTSE 100 – 6,150

'Father, forgive them, for they know not what they do.'
Luke 23: 34

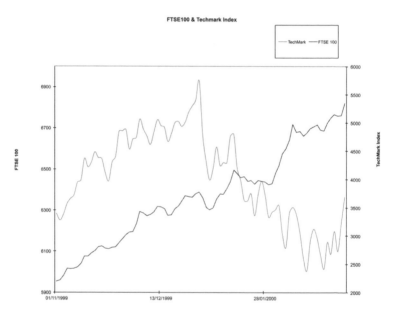

**Figure 2**

The chart above says it all. The vast majority of managed portfolios have suffered a vicious bear market in the last six months – one of the worst since the Second World War, bar 1974. Stocks have been down more than 38% – that includes such core groups as breweries, banks, property, utilities, retailers, even pharmaceuticals (off 30%) and virtually all

46

manufacturing, the core of most portfolios. To rub salt in the wound the new Techmark index has doubled since its intro- duction last November – a mere four months – and those who have been in IT since the beginning of last year have mostly trebled their paper money.

This phenomenon is not peculiar to the UK. It is almost the same in Europe, Japan and Korea and Hong Kong. One day last week the main Korean index fell 8%; that same day the KOSDAC index rose 8%. The KOSDAC index is exclusively for IT and new high-tech start-up companies.

Whitbread, with profits of £338 million and sales of $3 billion is about to be replaced in the FTSE 100 index by Baltimore Technologies with sales of £42 million, and losses of £32 million. It now has a market capitalisation of £4 bil- lion, having risen 6,000% in the last 12 months.

The pressure to jump on the IT bandwagon, and pay for it by ditching old blue chips, which have let the institutions down in terms of stock market price movement compared to the tech stocks, is so powerful that all but the strongest willed are now joining in the scramble.

Barclays' brokers who handle upwards of 200,000 deals a day from the public say that most of the buying is for tech- related stocks and most of the selling is of former blue chips to raise the money. The Jeremiahs, who have been warning for 12 months or longer that IT is overvalued, are no longer listened to. They have been wrong for too long, and fund managers who refused to buy leading IT stocks such as Sage, Logica, Misys, and Vodafone last year at 60 x earnings, 'because they were too expensive', are now eating their words and happily or reluctantly filling their portfolios with them at nearer 150 x earnings. The enthusiasts say, 'This time it's different.'

According to Sir John Templeton, one of the world's consistently shrewd investors, those are the four most expensive words to listen to in investment history.

[*Hardly had the PEP money rolled in than the first serious crack in the tech boom happened on Wall Street towards the end of March – London followed soon after.*]

## Market and Currency Update – 1 April
FTSE 100 – 6,540

The current (or should I say recent?) technology share boom is hauntingly reminiscent of the 'emerging markets' share boom of 1994. The same arguments were used to justify both stock market booms.

The basic argument for 'emerging markets' was that between 1992 and 1994 the 'old economies' of the world – UK, Western Europe, Japan and the USA – were ex-growth; there was surplus manufacturing capacity of virtually everything you like to mention from motor cars to bags of cement. The affluent communities living in these economies were already groaning under the weight of television sets, fridges, three-piece suites, and all the other household clutter of excessive consumerism.

By contrast the 'emerging markets' lacked nearly everything, and represented almost unlimited demand growth.

With the collapse of the Berlin Wall there also arrived a whole new universe of emerging economies at last in a political position to grow.

It was a very easy story to sell, and, superficially anyway, looked extremely convincing. So every fund management group in town launched an emerging markets fund, siphoning off billions of dollars and pounds from a willing and indeed eager investment public. Six years later only a handful of these funds are actually now worth their issue price.

So between November and early March the weight of money pouring into the tech sector with a limited supply of shares has sent them through the roof.

What will turn it over? And is the high-tech fall-out of the last three weeks the beginning of a collapse that will eventually knock between 50 and 75% off the participants, as happened in the emerging markets?

This new boom is taking place essentially in the advanced modern economies of Europe, Japan and the USA. They certainly do not suffer from lack of financial and legal infrastructure to handle the influx of cash to the sector. The new issues raised will end up building some of the companies of the future, not going into somebody's Swiss bank account (as rather too often happened in some of the more sleazy emerging market money-raising operations).

However, at the fringes we have already seen that human greed can operate within the regulatory framework in advanced economies, and have the same deadly effect on investor sentiment as the outright theft that occurred in some emerging markets.

Morgan Stanley, having spent six months with their top analytical teams assessing the correct market value for 'lastminute.com', then, at the 'last minute', for no better reason than the grey market was indicating a much higher start price, raised the issue price substantially. The result has been the first nail in the coffin of the dot-com boom as furious small investors feel deceived out of their expected profit, and as they are almost all registered with lastminute.com, that company has upset 200,000 customers overnight.

One cheeky investor apparently rang lastminute.com's helpline on the morning of the issue and said, 'You specialise in last minute offers, can you get me some of your own shares "last minute"?' The investor then said that the guy at the other end of the phone, instead of offering him shares, tried to sell him a 'last minute' holiday. Or he thought that was what he was offering, when he replied: 'Go to hell!'

The problem is that valuations in much of the TMT area (technology, media and telephone) are 90% sentiment and

10% value. If sentiment sours or is soured by unfriendly investor events (that's a polite way of saying 'rip-offs'!) then the capacity to lose money on current valuations is almost limitless.

[*By 1 June we had had the first 30% plus crash in TMT followed by the inevitable technical rebound that occurs after a big sell-off. With experience one knows this is always a second get-out-of-jail (nearly free) card if you find yourself in one of these sell-offs.*]

## Market and Currency Update – 1 June
FTSE 100 – 6,470

*Danger ahead*

With the NASDAQ up 19% last week it is more than likely we have now seen the technical bounce that you always get in the early stages of a big bear market. By this I do not mean a general bear market; I mean a bear market in TMT stocks. Actually this may well be accompanied by a new bull market in what are absurdly called 'old economy stocks'.

The four charts below indicate the potential danger of the situation in terms of electronic and electrical equipment, information technology, hardware, software and computer services.

Institutions tend not to be sellers until they are forced to. According to Andrew Smithers, who writes regularly in the *Evening Standard*, most fund managers he has spoken to recently are 'bearish', but none of them has dared sell, because the penalty for selling and being wrong for as little as three months could mean your job, or the loss of an account to your firm. Therefore it is safer to stay with the market, as, provided everyone goes down together and nobody does worse than anybody else, you will not be singled out for failure.

But of course what happens eventually is that when the sector really starts to slide the pressure to change horses mounts. The opposite happened in the last six months between October 1999 and March 2000. The rise and rise of the TMT stocks finally sucked in every institution there was because they couldn't dare any longer to be left out.

Once, however, the selling does start, everybody joins in quickly because they do not wish to be the only one left with a load of shares that are falling.

The problem is that the mathematics of the TMT sector make it look really vulnerable. Warren Buffet recently pointed this out. His argument for not joining the TMT bandwagon was that valuations were already so high that they were anticipating future earnings of more than $800 million a year for several hundred new companies within five years. Over the previous 20 years, he pointed out, on average only 10 new companies a year in the USA have been able to join the prestigious 400 organisations that currently earn $800 million or more a year.

So over a five year period there are likely to be about 50 new companies coming into this category. When there are over 500 companies valued already at a level that pre-supposes they will reach the magic $800 million earnings figure, then the odds are ten to one against.

The downside risk in the TMT sector still looks dangerously high. Common sense suggests that the so-called 'new economy' in spite of recent falls remains a danger zone. The so-called 'old economy', whilst offering value for money at the present level, may have significant upside potential, especially if the institutional investors at some point in the summer decide to jump ship from TMT.

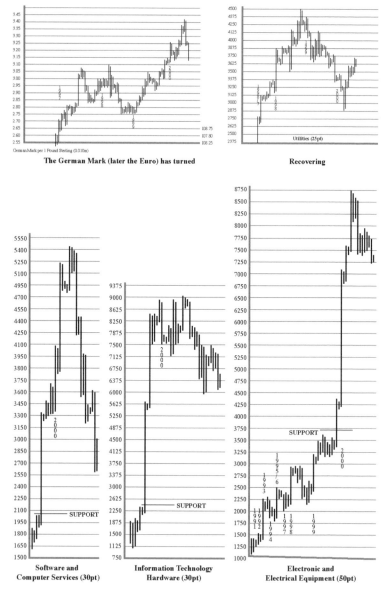

The German Mark (later the Euro) has turned

Recovering

Figures 3, 4 & 5

52

## Market and Currency Update – 1 August
FTSE 100 – 6,375

*Dad's Army hits back – TMT still very vulnerable*

The California technology letter, which has an amazing record for its in-house technology funds, states in every copy the following [updated]:

> The Dow currently sells at 63.3 x dividends (a yield of just 1.58%). At market bottoms the Dow sells at 17 x dividends, and will again at the bottom of the next bear market. At 22.4 x earnings the DJIA is still above the high end of its historic PE multiple range, in spite of its decline this year.

Only for the second time in recent years, the California technology letter team has decided to go 100% liquid in their two model technology portfolios. This occurred a fortnight ago when the NASDAQ had its big recovery from the April fall back to 4,000. In February this year it went liquid for the first time. The reason on this second occasion was that investors were still too bullish, and at 178 x earnings it was still very high, although somewhat cheaper than the 245 x earnings of its February peak!

For the last 20 years stock markets in Europe and the USA have been rising faster than underlying profits. This has been brought about by rising valuations for the same set of underlying profit performances. But in the last nine months, though the overall level of valuation has remained unchanged, the composition has altered drastically. A massive fall in the valuations of 'old economy' stocks has been compensated for by a quite grotesque supercharged valuation of 'tech' stocks.

The recent 'tech' fall-out has only really hit the 'tech'

smaller company sector – the preserve of private investors, who quickly took on board that the silly valuations were unsustainable once the balloon went up, and have subsequently dumped their stock. But these 250- and 350-index stocks all thrown together don't represent more than 10% of the market cap of Vodafone AirTouch. So their demise has had little impact on the main indices. Albeit on a valuation basis they are now beginning to represent interesting value.

By contrast the big tech stocks that account for 95% of the tech sector of the index – Reuters, Vodafone AirTouch, Sage, Sema, Logica, BT and, in Europe, Nokia, Ericsson, Telefónica, KPN Telecom and Alcatel – have dipped and recovered to within 10% to 30% of their all time highs of February. In the last few days, however, the rot has begun to set in: Deutsche Telekom, Europe's largest telecom company, has slumped from €60 to €28. The previously untouchable Nokia shocked the market with a profits hang up for its third quarter, and slumped 22% in a day, standing now at €47 against a high of €76. BT, £15 last February, is now lingering at 850p, as even the purblind institutional fund managers are reluctantly waking up to the fact that the tech bandwagon has hit the buffers.

What is still holding up a large part of the big capitalisation high-tech sector in the UK and Europe is the collective behavioural reaction of the fund managers. They all missed the big tech boom, in the sense that they were all 'underweight' in the tech sector when it happened between October and December 1999; and then they plunged in at prices double or treble what they had refused to pay a year earlier when those prices were then judged too 'risky' – effectively creating the bubble of January to March 2000.

When the bubble burst in March/April 2000, many institutions were still underweight tech-wise, and they have been using the fall to get 'up to weight', a process in which any kind of fundamental thinking about the correct value to put on the potential growth has been completely suspended. This demonstrates the absurdity of holding 'benchmark weightings'. What is the point in holding a weighting in *The Titanic* when it is already sinking?

'Wisdom' rarely exists in a herd. We feel safer going to our graves together than surviving separately; and I cannot remember a time in London – now the world's biggest centre of fund management – when the 'herd' instinct has been more pronounced. Every institutional portfolio in London is now stuffed with Vodafone and Nokia.

An interesting book was written on herd behaviour by Gustave Le Bon in 1895 entitled: *The Crowd: A Study of the Popular Mind*. What he said back then is as true today: 'Any individual when alone can be a cultivated person. Put him in a crowd and he becomes a blockhead.'

But analysts at Warburgs were only last week recommending Vodafone AirTouch with a target price of 500p (current price 290p). At 500p Vodafone's market capitalisation would be £500 billion, equivalent to 40% of the UK's total GDP. Pie in the sky? Or perhaps 'tulip in a mania'?

[*It was extraordinary just how long it took for the big institutions to finally see how stupid they were being, both holding and continuing to maintain 'weight' in the still absurdly overvalued tech sector. It left a wonderful opportunity for those who had been riding the tiger, and knew the ride was over, to get off a second time relatively unharmed. After all, three years later Vodafone was valued at 100p (previously 290p), BT at 200p (previously 850p), Reuters at £4 (previously £10), and Ericsson at SEK (Swedish krona) 17 (previously SEK 120).*]

## Market and Currency Update – 1 December

One might reasonably ask who or what is responsible for the tech boom going so 'bust' in a mere six months in so-called 'mature' markets? This is the sort of holocaust you expect to happen in Russia, or some similar unregulated cowboy economy, not one served with investment advice by the world's so-called greatest financial brains.

The main answer is all too simple: the level of professional advice handed out by the big fund management companies has been quite appalling. Not once during the boom did any of them murmur a warning that the growth potential had become very exaggerated by the stock price explosion. Last week Morgan Stanley Dean Witter suggested that valuations were vulnerable in some tech areas! Nice news for those who had already seen their shares drop 75%.

Clearly, when back in the spring the ten biggest tech companies' market capitalisation exceeded comfortably the combined GDP of The Netherlands and Switzerland, the tech sector was in a similar situation to when the Japanese Emperor's garden was (at the height of the Tokyo property boom of 1988) valued at more than the state of California. That turned out to be a prelude to a 12-year bear market in Japan (The Toppix main Japanese stock market index is still only at 14,500 against the 39,000 peak).

Let us hope that the bursting of this bubble does not bring the same extended misery on the western bourses. The charts below are all similar and the patterns are all terrible, indicating further falls before any serious resistance level is found. [*Indeed that is what later played out.*]

2000

**ARM Holdings**

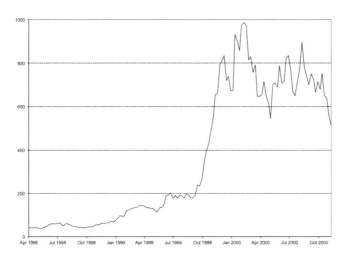

**Figure 6**

**Logica**

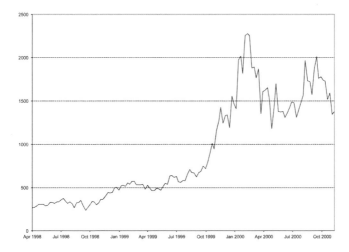

**Figure 7**

57

# THE NEWSLETTERS

Psion

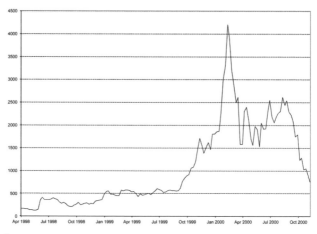

**Figure 8**

Sage Group

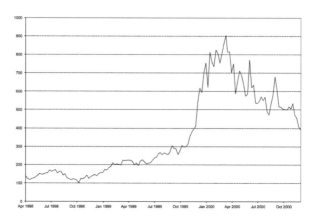

**Figure 9**

# 7

## *2001*

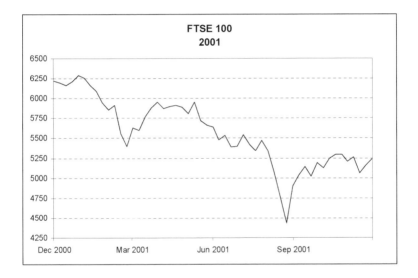

**Figure 10**

## Market and Currency Update – 1 January
FTSE 100 – 6,222

*All Together Now*

This was the title of an excellent book on management by Sir John Harvey-Jones, but it could just as well be the title for

59

the behaviour of the money managing institutions in the City last year. Not that they were much better the year before. But the frenzy surrounding the Internet accelerated a trend of 'unison' in investment behaviour, which has now virtually precluded any independent thought whatever from the fund managers.

What has happened is that the investing public, who have entrusted their savings to the big financial institutions via their unit trusts, PEPs, ISAs and pension funds, have become passive cannon fodder, who suffer the losses at the invest-ment front, whilst the bosses feast on ever more obscene bonuses, protected by their 'all together now' unanimity of advice.

Relative performance doesn't suffer if everybody does the same thing, however stupid. So in March last year the public was well and truly stuffed with that year's ISA allocation put into technology funds, as every leading institution pumped them out, took the fat fees, and left the public to nurse the 50% + losses six months later.

But 'relative' performance has so taken over City thinking that analysts have almost ceased to make any value judge-ments at all. The amazing result is that not one of the top ten performing shares in the FTSE 100 in the year 2000 – such as GUS, BAT, Sun Alliance, Thames Water and Tesco – ever got a serious recommendation from leading analysts.

Instead, analysts stuck with the TMT theme as it sank, encouraging investors to go on buying on the dips into BT, Sage, Sema, Marconi, Ericsson, Psion and so on. Practically without exception every one of these shares has ended the year at a new low, the highlight of the analysts' year being the strong recommendation to take up new shares in the German government's second sales round of Deutsche Telekom at 60 euros in July. They are now at 20 euros. Of course the fees, as usual, for raising the money meant astronomical bonuses to look forward to, and have no relation to the outcome.

More sinister is the announcement by the investment houses employed to relaunch Orange mobile for France Telecom in the spring of 2001 that no independent research company outside the launching consortium will be given access to the company's figures and projections unless that research is submitted for approval to the consortium before publication. In other words, if any independent investment analyst dares to produce a critical assessment of the new Orange business prospects, it will be suppressed – unless of course it is done without access to the company's information, in which case the managing consortium can 'rubbish' it on the grounds that the assessors are NOT in possession of the facts.

[*This was a very sinister development and showed how far the investment banks – freed by the repeal of Glass-Steagall – felt they could exercise market manipulation with impunity. Such conduct should have immediately been investigated by the regulators. Where were they?*]

Let us hope that there will be some leading institutions that take a stand on behalf of us, 'the cannon fodder public', and refuse to subscribe under such circumstances.

So we go into the New Year with the knowledge that frankly very few recommendations coming from the big institutions are likely to be a useful guide to wise investment, and that the issuing houses (which are driven by self-interest) should be watched like a hawk.

As for the consensus for next year, the eleven leading institutions predict that the FTSE 100 will rise to around 7,200. That is the consensus. Don't bank on it.

It is unnerving that the only other serious prediction, from David Schwarz, the well regarded stock market historian, is a warning that the likeliest historical analogies are pointing to a second 'down' year for the FTSE in 2001.

**TECHNICAL ANALYSIS From Richard Lake**          1st **December 2000**

(Richard Lake was chief technical analyst at Brewin Dolphin Securities at the time)

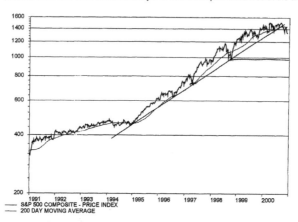

S&P 500 COMPOSITE - PRICE INDEX
200 DAY MOVING AVERAGE

### Standard & Poor's 500 Composite index now 1,314.95

I sent this ten-year chart to you in October. The subsequent fall to 1,340, rally to 1,435 and then more recent decline only reinforces the idea that a major top formation has developed. As you can see, the index is now decisively below its main uptrend line and the 200 day moving average which is now falling. Technically, the Standard & Poor's Composite index suggests that Wall Street has started a bear market. However, do not despair. There will still be many US stocks continuing to rise and outperform.

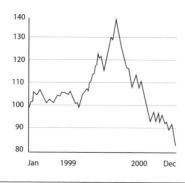

**Figure 11**

## Market and Currency Update – 1 February
FTSE 100 – 6,292 (1 Jan – 6,222)

*All apart now!*

Thirty years ago the City was a very individualistic place, largely because the dissemination of information was difficult and slow. It was not easy to find out what other people were doing, so each investment firm followed its instincts and expertise to uncover value that others might not know about. There was much more genuine diversity of investment approach and opinion. Nowadays, due to the instant transmission of every form of information, everybody knows what everyone else is thinking almost before they have thought it, and the effect is to make analysts and fund managers cluster together to draw like-minded conclusions and make like-minded decisions for fear of being the odd one out. This conformity of behaviour, reaching its *summa cum laude* in the index tracker, apart from being destabilising to financial assets generally, ends up producing a lousy investment performance. The forced buying of Vodafone last year by all the big funds, fearing to let their 'weightings' in the FTSE 100 telecoms get out of line, has led, from this share alone, to about a 3% underperformance compared to the few who ignored such nonsense.

However, this very herd-like behaviour gives exceptional opportunities to the independent thinker. The market gets it wrong more often and by a wider margin than in the past, as it got it terribly wrong last year in the 'serial' overvaluation of TMT stocks. Some clever, and lucky, hedge fund managers have doubled their money this year by 'shorting' TMT stocks and exploiting the market's extreme failure (short term) to evaluate their potential correctly.

Luckily, in spite of the current government's efforts to control us all from Alastair Campbell's 'Spin Kingdom' (or from Brussels), we still live in really free financial markets, and free markets always adjust to reality in the end.

More than perhaps for a long time, this year promises to be a real 'market of stocks' rather than a stock market, with quite significant numbers of shares doing rather well, and other sectors continuing to do very poorly. The independent minded managers could have a very good year; the herd managers, another poor one.

So which sectors are likely to do well in 2001? Let's start with TMT. People believe that 'technology' is the future, therefore one must invest in it. This, however, is a complete *non sequitur* – if the price is wrong you should not invest.

The 'T' of TMT looks to be much the most dangerous area, with further significant downward adjustment of share values likely, ending finally when there is a high profile bankruptcy. Of the potential candidates, even BT is not exempt, being arguably the weakest managed of all the big telecoms. Due to the boom and perceived future meteoric growth of data transmission, hugely excessive amounts of equity capital and bank debt have created a monster glut in telephone systems. Price pressure is now so extreme that many tariffs have dropped 90%, wiping out any chance for most of these investments ever to show a return.

If the phone companies can't make the money then the whole chain backwards is in trouble: Marconi, Nortel, Ericsson, Cisco, and the technology licensors – Psion, ARM, Bookham and so on. Conclusion: Don't be sucked in by the recent price falls – AVOID!

Now to the software companies and systems creators and operators. These technology companies have fallen out of bed along with the rest. There is not the same surplus capacity, and the latent demand is enormous. Many stocks in this sector are now on recession ratings.

Now the old economy. All the big fund managers are now presenting themselves as 'value' investors. Last year they were all 'tech experts'. There is danger in this sector particularly in the very defensive stocks, like food companies, with very slow long-term growth. They are not worth a high PE. They got too cheap but there is a very definite ceiling to their potential value. They will be quickly dumped by investors when the more exciting areas of the economy pick up steam again. But the so-called old economy represents over 80% of all human activity.

The potential in smaller companies generally has been enhanced by the arrival of the Internet. For the first time ever they can access the world without the expense of a global physical network.

PS. Lloyds' bid for Abbey National is the last gasp of a tired management that has run out of ideas. Lloyds has lost its magic – sell!

[*The Lloyds bid for Abbey was a good example of how investors can get an early alert that a company has started to lose its way. In this case the clue was a board action that looked obviously unwise. Luckily the bid failed because subsequent accountancy revelations at Abbey revealed that the company was nearly insolvent. Its market capitalisation then crashed, and Santander stepped in, in timely fashion (as good timing as Lloyds had been bad), and bought up the network and the best pieces for a song.*

*By March 2001 the full awfulness of the over-capacity situation in many areas of the tech industry had well and truly dawned on the market. The sector had not found a bottom, and there was nothing in sight to suggest it would soon. Almost the entire sector had succumbed to Barton Biggs syndrome: 'There is no asset class that cannot be destroyed by too much capital.'*

*And the tech sector had received an awesome bundle of excess capital by any standards.*]

## Market and Currency Update – 1 March
FTSE 100 – 5,902

Once upon a time there was a shepherd, who tended his sheep in a most isolated area. Suddenly a brand new Cherokee Jeep appears in a cloud of dust and stops directly in front of him. The driver jumps out of the Jeep wearing a Brioni suit, Gucci shoes, Ray Ban sun-glasses and an Armani tie, and asks: 'When I guess how many sheep you have can I have one?' The shepherd looks at the young man and then at his peacefully grazing sheep and says quietly, 'Why not?' The young man parks his Jeep, connects his electronic notebook with his mobile phone, goes onto the Internet to the NASA site, scans the area with help from his GPS satellite navigator system, opens a data bank with 60 Excel tables and oodles of formulae. Finally he prints out a 50-page report from his high-tech mini printer, turns around to the shepherd and says: 'You have exactly one thousand five hundred and eighty-six sheep.'

The shepherd says, 'That's correct, go ahead and pick one.' The young man takes one and puts it into his Jeep. The shepherd looks at him and says: 'Can I have my sheep back if I guess your profession?'

The young man answers: 'Sure, why not!'

The shepherd says: 'You are an equity analyst.'

'Wow that's correct, how did you know?'

'Easy,' says the shepherd, 'firstly, you come here even though nobody has asked you; secondly, you want a sheep as payment for something I already know; and finally, you have no clue what I actually do, since you picked my dog.'

There is actually a wealth of talent being misdirected by the top management of the 25 big fund managers, who now control 80% of the funds. The cry of a fund manager 12 months ago stating he was being forced to buy Vodafone at a price he knew was absurd in order to comply with maintaining the 'correct weighting' rings all too true.

Meanwhile stormy waters are building in the stock market and none more so than in the telecoms sector. There is no reason to believe the end is at hand either, other than in the terminal sense that one of the big telecoms companies will go to the wall. The chairman of Intel said the other day: '3G has bankrupted them.' And this brings us round to our old and bumbling friends –the commercial banks. They have lent £300 billion to telcos of all shapes and sizes. Of the supine British clearers, Barclays appears to be in poll position with the new CEO, Matt Barrett, saying he is 'throwing his weight' behind Barclays Capital, and highlighting its 'strong European franchise in the debt products needed to finance the enormous deals in telecoms, media and technology'! Barclays had to cut its dividend in 1992 after its binge of lending during the 1988–91 property 'boom to bust'. *Plus ça change*! Damage to portfolios as a result of the telco crash, and the return to earth in the rest of the IT sector, both here and in the US, is now so great that the chance of a major 'tech rally' in the near future, against a background of continuing profit warnings from that sector, appears to be waning by the minute.

**Market and Currency Update – 25 March**
FTSE 100 – 5,402 (1 Jan – 6,222)

The figures below (showing the performance of popular funds from major investment houses over the last six months) make clear the disappointing performance of the popular funds of major investment houses in the last six months.

| Fall in six months to 17 March – FTSE 100: | -11% |
|---|---|
| Fall excluding charges (for UK growth funds): | |
| Dresdner RCM Funds (UK) Ltd | -23.6% |
| Norwich Union | -20.83% |
| Gartmore | -20.70% |
| Barings | -19.8% |
| Scottish Widows | -19.20% |
| Merrill Lynch | -18.10% |
| Invesco GT | -18.00% |
| ABN AMRO | -17.15% |
| CGU | -16.40% |
| M&G (index tracker) | -13.85% |

**Figure 12**

It is an uncomfortable fact for these funds that since the FTSE 100 peaked at 6,910 at the end of December 1999, no less than 41 FTSE 100 stocks (nearly half) are currently higher than they were then. (I am indebted to Richard Lake, a leading UK chartist, who now works on behalf of Brewin Dolphin, for this data.)

So the professional stock-pickers not only picked the wrong stocks but were overweight in them – hence substantially underperforming against the FTSE 100 itself.

As this has all happened in a free market, investors will vote with their feet. Habits and behaviour within the industry will alter quickly; hence already the investor enthusiasm for hedge fund managers, because they are seen to be people who at least do their own thing for better or worse.

Now back to valuations and why current market levels are looking sensible. Let us first take the world's ten leading technology companies – those that will drive forward the world economy (see Fig. 13). These are the well established strong market leaders whose prices in the boom got very expensive, but did not go ballistic, unlike the fashionable newcomers – Cisco Systems, JDS Uniphase, Juniper Networks, Yahoo and so on. Some of this latter group with their mushroom growth may fail altogether, as management that is quickly stuck together over a short period unravels equally rapidly if the going gets really tough.

| | Price high | Price today | PE now |
|---|---|---|---|
| Microsoft | $115 | $50 | 27 |
| Intel | $75 | $24 | 16 |
| Applied Materials | $115 | $42 | 15 |
| IBM | $134 | $88 | 20 |
| Hewlett-Packard | $77 | $29 | 18 |
| Nortel | $123 | $26 | 23 |
| Ericsson | $25 | $5.5 | 44 |
| Nokia | $62 | $25 | 30 |
| Sun Micro | $64 | $17 | 35 |
| Sony | $141 | $65 | 30 |

Ericsson's high PE is due to losses in its mobile phone division.

**Figure 13**

Note: Vodafone is not included because it is a retailer. It is not a creator of technology. But it sells at 50 x. Vodafone is the last totem that has not yet toppled and in which all the institutions are 'fully weighted'; furthermore, none dare dump it, that is until, like Cable and Wireless (the other telecoms totem they all held) it announces a profits warning. [*It was not long before Vodafone too finally toppled and sank to 100p against its peak of 400p.*]

The other major worldwide technology companies are now back on historic PEs, where they represent serious value for money on their likely five-year forward growth. [*That turned out to be correct on all but two: Sony, which got into a further mess with its games consoles, and halved again; and Nortel Networks, which finally collapsed.*]

Meanwhile, so-called old economy stocks in Europe are still historically cheap as a result of the 'oversell' in 1999 and 2000 when European fund managers, having steered clear of technology for years, all went bonkers on it at once, and dumped the 'old' economy.

69

## DANGER OF 'LIVING IN CLOUD CUCKOO LAND'

# Gloom-laden conclusion on outlook for IT

**By Caroline Daniel,
IT Correspondent**

Revenue growth in the UK IT services and software sector fell to below 10 per cent last year, the first time since the recession of the early 1990s, and is unlikely to improve this year, according to an Ovum Holway report on the sector to be published later this week.

The gloomy conclusion about prospects for the sector comes in the report written by Richard Holway, an independent analyst of the IT sector.

"As in previous slowdowns, this had a greater effect on profits, which actually declined by a massive 86 per cent in 2000 – the biggest fall on record," Mr Holway said.

"I think we will continue to see profit warnings this year, especially from companies involved with systems integration."

The analysis contrasts with the more upbeat comments from many European IT services companies, such as Logica and CMG.

Last week CMG, the Anglo-Dutch group, expressed confidence that its biggest customers would increase their spending with CMG by more than 10 per cent this year.

Mr Holway also dismissed hopes that demand for IT services would rebound next year.

Instead, he predicts that demand from 2002-2004 will remain modest.

"I don't buy it. Every time there has been a rebound before it has been associated with a technology revolution. In the early 1980s demand was led by the introduction of the PC. In the early 1990s it was led by Windows, and in the late 1990s, by the internet and e-commerce boom."

He added: "there will be no big technology shift before 2004, and anyone who believes Europe will be immune to the US slowdown is living in cloud cuckoo land." In spite of that analysis, the report said there are some areas where growth is likely to be strong in the IT sector, such as outsourcing.

"In any downturn people look to outsourcing as a way to cap costs. We have seen some of the biggest-ever outsourcing contracts recently, with some global contracts worth more than £20m a year," Mr Holway said. The companies which have benefited most from that trend are big companies, such as IBM Global services and EDS, which were the two biggest IT services providers in the UK last year. Mid-sized companies are likely to struggle to win these deals.

Another area which could buck the downward trend in demand is the public sector. That could benefit companies such as Torex, which targets the healthcare industry, or RM, an education specialist, the report said.

*The 2001 Holway Report is produced by Ovum Holway, £6,000. 01252 740900*

**Figure 14**

70

## Market and Currency Update – 17 July

*When to buy the techs?*

The short answer is: 'Not yet and not here.'

The tech industry worldwide is facing its worst recession since 1986. The combination of extra millennium 2000 work with the arrival of the Internet concertinaed about four years' work into two, leading to a one-off boom in margins and profits for virtually all areas of the industry, as a 'must-have-regardless-of-cost' frenzy gripped business everywhere. Business is now licking its wounds, realising how much money it has wasted on overpriced tech products and services. Subsequently it has gone from 'must have' to 'only if it is essential'. This in itself was exacerbated by booming tech equities, which led, particularly in the telecoms sector, to effortless raising of vast amounts of excess capital, which has created a horrendous surplus of capacity in this industry.

It is estimated that the number of fibre optic networks laid across Europe, in the lettable space terms of the City of London, is equivalent to the construction of nine Canary Wharfs. 'Wits' are now saying that alleged sea level rise is not due to global warming, but to the number of cables piling up on the ocean floors.

Whilst the established retailers of telecom services, the old former national companies, at least have a large client base usually still captive in the local loop, the new companies have nothing to compete on other than price, which has crumbled so much that all these capital projects are deeply under water. Those financed by debt have little or no hope. The established companies – BT, France Telecom, Deutsche Telekom, Telefónica – will totter on, with falling profits and reduced or disappearing dividends for some years until capacity is taken out by merger and bankruptcy, and prices firm up – probably five years away. Meanwhile in spite of their falls, many of these companies are still selling on lofty multiples of their reduced earning capacity. This is now a contraction industry in terms of profits, not a growth industry, but is not yet priced as such. The correct price for BT must be between £2 and £3 at the most. Its outlook is far worse than four years ago when it was selling at £4.

When it comes to the supply companies, the situation is dire. The US has recognised this with Nortel, down from $80 to $8 and still heading south as order books dry up. Somebody is going to go to the wall. The most likely candidate must be the weakest technologically, and that is Marconi. But the others have several lean years ahead. The prospect, touted around by hallucinating analysts, of a pick-up in the fourth quarter, is ludicrous. And to hope that 3G will ride to the rescue is a mirage.

One of the problems in the UK investment management industry is that benchmarking sucked the entire fund management universe into tech shares, which they never understood (this is why fund managers had always avoided them in the past). And now they are stuck with them they cannot conceptually grasp just what a mess there is out there. And the analysts – equally shell-shocked by the devastation of their former glory – dare not say, 'I'm a fool, get out! The ship is sinking.' Our in-house telecoms analyst keeps advising that Nokia and Vodafone are a safe port in the storm – but he cannot accept that the storm is in 'the port' as well!

Trust the charts. They have been unerringly correct for 18 months on the techs. The downward trend lines have never been breached by the rallies, and these have always faded, and new lows subsequently hit. The downward trend lines are still intact. And this applies in spades for Vodafone. Sell into the next rally. It is dead money.

The telecoms sector is in the direst state of all the tech areas. Software is going through a gruelling short-term

buyers' strike. Let the profit warnings work their way
through. They are likely to go on for at least two more
quarters.

In Europe, household computer penetration is lower and
older. All this will gradually come right, but the waiting will
sink a lot more Internet software companies. If you are not
sure which ones, it is better to keep away from the sector.

The 'chip' market is now alleged to be in structural surplus.
But has this not been said at the bottom of every 'chip'
recession? This area looks more promising.

[*Between April and August the dregs of the tech boom continued to unravel and the FTSE 100 fell 1,000 points. All in all
markets were looking much more reasonable but of course we
were not to know that Al-Qaeda were shortly to hijack four
civilian aircraft and fly two of them into the Twin Towers;
furthermore that this was going to lead to the second Iraq
War.*]

## Market and Currency Update – 1 August
FTSE 100 – 5,403

The chart below (Fig. 15) of the PE ratio on the UK market
shows the reason why equities did so well from 1980 through
to 2000. This is largely because the PE ratio went from 8 at
the beginning of this period to 22 by the end.

The chart also shows that the PE reached 22 in 1968 and
did not get back there until 40 years later (a sober thought for
those who joined the market for the first time in 1968 or for
that matter in 1999). It explains why the huge losses in
equities sustained since 1968 led to a period (from 1974
through to 1980) when 'investment advice' was consistently
cautious on equities (whereas with the benefit of hindsight it
should have been aggressive). Conversely, in the last 5 years –

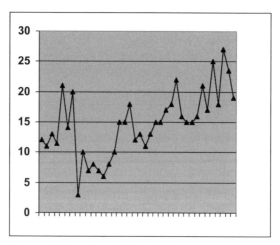

**Figure 15 PE ratio on UK market**

after 15 years of ever rising equity markets – the cult of the equity has become so entrenched that conventional 'good advice' is to favour equities as the best and obvious place for long-term investment.

The point is that taking a long stock market view – 70 years or more – price earnings of equities have averaged around 12 to 15. The higher they get, for whatever reason, above this norm, the more risky equity investment becomes.

So where are we now? First the PE on the FTSE 100 is likely to fall fast this year without the FTSE itself dropping, simply because the lofty PE components like Marconi, Spirent, Bookham, Autonomy, etc. are all dropping out, and will be replaced with so-called old economy companies on PEs of between 9 and 12x.

This gives one some hope that much of the equity adjustment that has taken place in the last year has once again put a big chunk of the market back onto a realistic PE rating, from which asset appreciation could begin again.

Nevertheless, as the reality of life buffets the 'cult of the equity', it is much more likely that we are moving into a

74

period where valuations of equities generally will be lower than in the recent past, and closer to the long-term norm. To some degree equity investment will be like climbing a descending escalator, and recently scorned assets such as fixed interest securities should again constitute a core part of any stock market investment strategy.

## Market and Currency Update – 1 September
FTSE 100 – 5,305

The fascinating thing about charts is that they usually reflect what 'real' money is doing rather than the theoretical ranting of financial analysts whose feet are all too often planted firmly in mid air.

Just under a year ago in the October 2000 newsletter, when the FTSE 100 was 6,350, the opening paragraph read: 'Garderenes head for the precipice,' followed by, 'One could say of the last twelve months (Oct 1999 to Oct 2000): never has so much been paid by so many for so little.' (The Garderenes were a herd of swine who all followed each other over a precipice.)

Without exception, all the technology charts at the time were showing the 'top' patterns that have historically proved so ominous. They have been absolutely correct:

| Stock | Price Oct 2000 | Price today |
|---|---|---|
| Vodafone | 280p | 135p |
| Marconi | 700p | 55p |
| ARM | 500p | 260p |
| Mysys | 650p | 280p |
| Spirent | 550p | 115p |
| Logica | 1600p | 700p |
| BT | 700p | 425p |
| Cable and Wireless | 850p | 330p |

**Figure 16**

75

Some of the bottom charts have been equally accurate:

| Stock | Price Oct 2000 | Price today |
|---|---|---|
| Unilever | 400p | 580p |
| Land Securities | 700p | 900p |
| Boots | 500p | 680p |
| Halifax | 550p | 800p |

**Figure 17**

So where from here? Firstly, waiting for pricked balloons to reinflate has seldom been a profitable exercise in the stock market. Most of the above collapsed companies are still on a high earnings yield, minimum dividend (Vodafone 1%), and in the telecom sector there is such a glut of capacity that future earnings recovery seems very distant.

Many old economy stocks have had a big rise since the end of the tech boom, as institutions have been shifting back into them, and they are now back to the top of their old trading range (e.g. Unilever, BAA, Diago, Royal Bank of Scotland); but they are not unduly expensive depending on the size of the economic downturn we are facing. It does seem very early in the downturn for them to break out into all time high ground.

It has always been right in the past to 'follow the Fed' (the Federal Reserve, central bank of the USA) when it drops interest rates sharply. Though it might be said that the very sharpness of the drop indicates some concern by the Fed that it has quite a challenge on its hands.

The headline indices may still have some way to fall, but it is, and always has been, against this kind of background that real value can be found at a price which should deliver both good income and prospects of capital gain over time.

## Market and Currency Update – 1 October
FTSE 100 – 4,901 (1 Sep – 5,335)

*[This was just after the terrible collapse of the Twin Towers in New York.]*

Firstly, one's limitless sympathy goes out to those who suffered an unspeakable death in the infamy of September 11, and to their families and friends who will endure the terrible pain for so long after. Respect for their memory can only be expressed in the hope that their sacrifice will not be in vain. As Edmund Burke once stated: 'When bad men combine, the good must associate; else they will fall one by one, an unpitied sacrifice in a contemptible struggle.'

The sheer enormity of the outrage may in fact be the downfall of the evil perpetrators, as it is already bringing together a near worldwide coalition against them, stretching across all religions and cultures.

Even in those parts of the world where murder and assassination remain a regular method of either seizing or maintaining political power, such indiscriminate killing of totally innocent and unconnected human beings goes way over the line of any kind of acceptable conduct.

Hence support for President Bush's campaign to deal with this type of terrorism is coming from leaders and peoples who do not normally see eye to eye with western values. With this sort of consensus against the atrocity and its perpetrators, there must be a much higher chance of bringing them and their accomplices to justice.

Markets discount what they can see, and in the aftermath of September 11 they saw a real recession coming, as general loss of confidence would hit an already overstretched consumer.

To the extent that what is discounted is already in the price, the risk of the market falling further from that point was low. Indeed in the last week, as the success of the coalition build up around the world against terrorism has emerged, the market has already rallied somewhat. Clearly the sooner the general terrorism threat is seen to be being tackled effectively, so economic revival will appear more imminent, and current stock market prices will seem undervalued.

The other powerful force that should help overcome the recession is the almost universally low rate of inflation in the advanced economies. This gives much greater scope to the central banks to risk stimulative monetary policies to avert recession. Even that dummy, the European Central Bank, has belatedly woken up to its responsibilities.

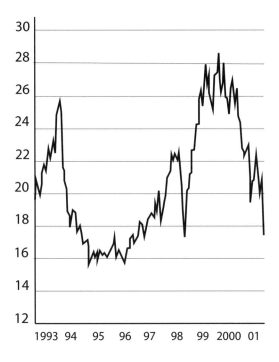

**Figure 18**

78

Price earnings ratios have fallen sharply and were getting close to historic average levels. This meant further equity risk on any medium-term outlook was now reasonable.

[*This was a time when one had to make sure that clients did not sell their equities just because of the panic induced by the September 11 atrocity. Historically gut panics caused by unexpected political events repair themselves within two or three months. By December the market had recovered all those losses.*]

## Market and Currency Update – 1 November
FTSE 100 – 5,010

*The equity risk/reward*

A very interesting paper was delivered by Professor Richard Sylla (Henry Kaufman Professor of the History of Financial Institutions and Markets at New York University) at a conference organised by the Stewart Ivory Foundation this October in Edinburgh. It was entitled: 'Tulip Mania to Dot-Com Hysteria; What Can We Learn From Past Financial Cycles?'

The professor's chart (see Figs 19, 20) shows that over a 200-year period the US stock market has delivered an average annual inflation-adjusted 6.6% return, whereas the bond market has delivered an average 3.12% return – inflation adjusted.

Since none of us have yet mastered immortality, 200 years is too long a period over which to judge an investment decision. For most investors the likely lifespan of their investment horizon would be a maximum of 25 years (for some a 'week' is stretching it). But to achieve the average performance for equities over 25 years is infinitely more hazardous than over 200 years. Simply by using the charts one can see how dramatically the performance can vary over a ten-year period:

| | |
|---|---|
| 1910 to 1920 | -5% per annum (£100,000 becomes £63,000) |
| 1964 to 1974 | -5% per annum (ditto, inflation adjusted) |

**Figure 19**

By contrast, if you had entered the market with £100,000 in either of the following decades your return would have been significant:

| | |
|---|---|
| 1918 to 1928 | +17% (£100,000 becomes £370,000) |
| 1988 to 1998 | +15% (£100,000 becomes £240,000) |

**Figure 20**

But of course if you held on till 1931 or till 2003, 90% or so of the profits vanish – how dangerous overvalued markets can be!

It all depends on the PE when you start and when you get out. As you can see from the professor's charts we have recently ended a 20-year wealth creating period in equities where the average PE had gone from 8.5 in 1980 to 20 + in the year 2000, making it, in the process, an extremely profitable equity market. It is also atypical, because it has been one of the longest periods of equity outperformance, spanning almost an entire generation. Indeed, there is hardly anybody around now in investment management who would remember the decade from 1964 to 1974 during which the majority of investors lost money.

Has the recent set-back, bringing the market back from a PE of 24 to 17.9, been sufficient to achieve a long-term return above the average? Answering this question brings us to the problem of averages, and we have to decide whether the preponderant influence of large capitalisation companies in recent years has made averages meaningless for large numerical parts of the market (by numerical I mean the number of companies represented rather than the market capitalisation).

> FTSE 100 currently 85% of market capitalisation of All-Share
> FTSE 250 currently 14% ditto
> Small capitalisation currently 5% ditto

**Figure 21**

It so happens that the PE of the small caps is currently a mere 10 x and the PE of the 250 just 15.5 x. If you take these out of the equation of the FTSE All-Share index then the FTSE 100 is trading on 18.9 x not 15 x for the whole market. This looks somewhat more expensive and less attractive in the long term. It also shows that the average market PE only refers to a small part of the economy in terms of number of companies, and completely conceals the fact that other large groups of companies have a very different and much lower average. So effectively in market capitalisation terms 85% of the market is on a PE of 18.9 x.

Professor Sylla has taken just one market, the US, but we have a number of different markets to choose from. For instance, Japan has displayed a totally different cycle to the USA. Since 1989 it has been downhill all the way from 39,000 on the Japanese main market index to current 10,000 in 2001. In the same period the S&P 500 index has gone from 500 to 2,500, but the PE argument holds. In 1989 the S&P 500 stood at an attractive, below historical average, 14 x; and the Nikkei Index Japan stood at a crazy 67 x. Anybody following the principle of only investing in shares when the index of the particular market is below its 200-year moving average would have waved goodbye to Japan and shifted to the USA with spectacular results. One has risen nearly 5 x; the other fallen by 75%.

Today, however, the PE is still a vulnerable figure. The current US stock market value is double the replacement cost of assets it is composed of.

In conclusion, if there is a lesson to learn from stock market history it is to avoid high PEs, whether in individual shares or entire markets. They spell doom.

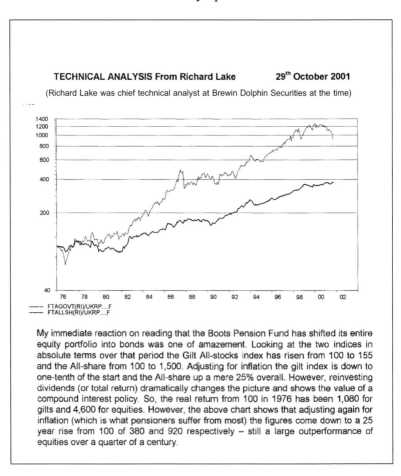

**TECHNICAL ANALYSIS From Richard Lake        29<sup>th</sup> October 2001**

(Richard Lake was chief technical analyst at Brewin Dolphin Securities at the time)

— FTAGOVT(RI)/UKRP....F
······ FTALLSH(RI)/UKRP....F

My immediate reaction on reading that the Boots Pension Fund has shifted its entire equity portfolio into bonds was one of amazement. Looking at the two indices in absolute terms over that period the Gilt All-stocks index has risen from 100 to 155 and the All-share from 100 to 1,500. Adjusting for inflation the gilt index is down to one-tenth of the start and the All-share up a mere 25% overall. However, reinvesting dividends (or total return) dramatically changes the picture and shows the value of a compound interest policy. So, the real return from 100 in 1976 has been 1,080 for gilts and 4,600 for equities. However, the above chart shows that adjusting again for inflation (which is what pensioners suffer from most) the figures come down to a 25 year rise from 100 of 380 and 920 respectively – still a large outperformance of equities over a quarter of a century.

**Figure 22 The quarter century when it was right to be in equities**

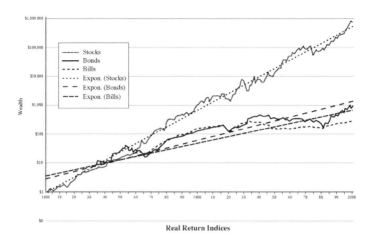

Figure 23

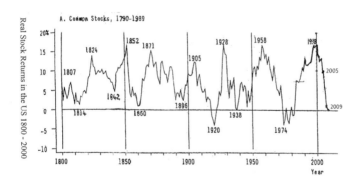

Figure 24

83

# 8

## *2002*

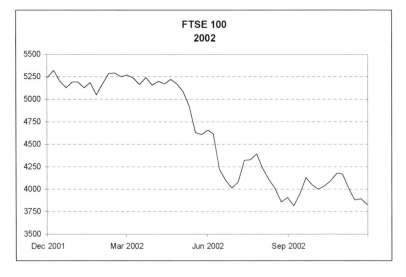

**Figure 25**

*[2002 was the year that a serious bear market occurred. This was partly due to the Twin Tower outrage turning into the second Iraq War, and partly because of the still somewhat above average PE of leading markets that were vulnerable to such a dramatic political upheaval.]*

## Market and Currency Update – 1 January
FTSE 100 – 5,242 (30 Dec)

The new investment fashion is the hedge fund, currently being offered by every manager in town; a good reason in itself to avoid them.

It is all part of the herd complex that continues to undermine London as a leading fund management centre. It was a world leader up until about five years ago, with British managed funds outperforming their peers in most parts of the world. But particularly in the last three years, this pre-eminence has collapsed due to a conscious policy of 'benchmarking' and nearly everybody losing their heads in the tech boom.

Benchmarking is the negation of intelligent capital allocation, and intelligent capital allocation is what our industry is supposed to be about.

Regarding the so-called UK growth funds of the leading investment houses, everybody has the same top holdings: Vodafone at 8.6%, BP at 7.6%, Glaxo at 6.8%, HSBC at 5.5%, RBS at 4.4% and AstraZeneca at 3.4%. (Looking back 18 months it would include Marconi at 3.3%.)

These weightings are almost an exact replica of the FTSE 100 index weightings, which you can shadow yourself for 0.25% annual cost in a tracker fund.

We are likely to see some substantial changes taking place both in fund management and in portfolio composition, with property and fixed interest assuming a more important role, some time soon.

So what does 2002 hold in store? Well last year I suggested that the sole soothsayer who might be right was David Schwartz, the stock market historian, who predicted that the market would fall by the end of the year from the then level of 6,000. Every single major investment house predicted that the market would end higher, from Schroders to HSBC. Only Warburg was pretty cautious and even they predicted a higher level. Everybody was wrong by more than 1,000 points except for David Schwartz.

This year the optimism is somewhat stronger, the popular argument being that an economic rebound will lead, as it always has done, to higher markets, and that after an unprecedented two 'down' years the market is bound to rise.

I'm afraid that while I would like this to happen I believe it won't. We may face another year of falling markets.

The FTSE 100 sells currently on a PE of 20.1 and a yield of 2.58%. Historically this valuation is still near the top end of the cycle. In 1980 the PE of the FTSE 100 was 8. The long-term median is 15.

Let's suppose that far from a re-rating of profits, there is a continued de-rating down towards the long-term norm. Nobody seems even to consider this. But it looks considerably more likely than a re-rating. Fixed interest offers 5–6% guaranteed, and property probably 6–8%.

Can new money afford to risk a third year of negative returns? Old habits die hard and fund managers will do everything they can to lure the money to the equity market, as fixed interest investment is far less profitable and property investment is usually outside their compass. (When Boots switched its pension fund from equities to fixed interest its annual running costs fell from £10 million to £250,000.)

But the credibility of these people is now doubly suspect, because not only have they been wrong for nearly three years, but they made a complete hash of their TMT investments – going in much too late at much too high a price.

So there must be a doubt as to how much new money goes into equities in 2002. Ratings are historically stretched, the charts of the big solid companies look ominous (see Fig. 26), and the economic recovery is certainly not yet in the bag.

But only bear markets produce the real bargains. The low after September 11 of 4,433 should hold. If the market fell back near this level in 2002 then such a double bottom could be the strong indicator of the new bull market. But it will not be led by yesterday's stars: BT, Pearson, Logica, Nokia, Ericsson, Telefónica, Cisco Systems, etc. It never is.

New stars will rise, and with the still very modest valuations in the smaller company sector (ignored by the big institutions for too long), this area constitutes a hopeful hunting ground with real immediate returns.

# Survey finds hope of 14% Footsie rise

INVESTORS could see a 14% jump in the value of their portfolios during 2002, writes *Alicia Wyllie*.

A survey of five leading investment banks by The Sunday Times shows that analysts are expecting the FTSE 100 to end the year at between 5,500 and 6,000 points. That is a rise of between 258 and 758 points on Friday's close of 5,242.

The most bullish prediction comes from Morgan Stanley, which expects a 14% rise in the index over the year to about 6,000. It believes the market will reach this target in the first few months of the year, and then fluctuate around this level.

Slightly less optimistic is Credit Suisse, which is forecasting a 700-point rise to 5,900. UBS Warburg and HSBC are more cautious, predicting 5,750 and 5,700 respec-

tively, while Merrill Lynch comes in with the lowest figure of 5,500. Steve Russell, UK strategist at HSBC Investment Bank, says: "Equity markets will rise gradually in 2002, but the recovery will be subdued as low inflation acts as a drag on earnings."

However, as our table shows, analysts' predictions can be wildly inaccurate. At the start of 2001, Credit Suisse was forecasting that

the FTSE 100 would end the year at 7,100. While nobody could have foreseen the shock caused by the September 11 terrorist attacks, with hindsight this looks hopelessly optimistic.

Fears of recession in America, which had started to gather pace in September 2000, depressed the market early in the year. Even before the attacks, the Footsie was struggling to stay above 5,500.

UBS Warburg had the most bearish prediction for the FTSE 100 in 2001. It expected the index to end the year at 6,350, which was pretty conservative considering the Footsie reached 6,334 in January. In the event, even that proved too optimistic.

After September 11 the banks revised their forecasts. By the time markets closed on Friday, UBS Warburg was proved the most accurate of the five investment banks surveyed, having reduced its forecast to 5,250, just 8 points above the close of 5,242.

Michael Coleman of Redmayne-Bentley, a stockbroker, says 2002 will be marked by cautious optimism: "Investors should be poised for action as some shares will significantly outperform the market, but they should beware irrational euphoria."

## WHERE WILL THE FTSE 100 END UP?

| Bank | Prediction for 2001 | Revised figure | Prediction for 2002 |
|---|---|---|---|
| Credit Suisse | 7,100 | 5,350 | 5,900 |
| HSBC | 6,800 | 4,700 | 5,700 |
| Merrill Lynch | 6,600 | 4,900 | 5,500 |
| Morgan Stanley | 6,650 | 5,700 | 6,000 |
| UBS Warburg | 6,350 | 5,250 | 5,750 |

Figures revised in September

Figure 26

[*Markets generally were still looking pretty overvalued and the reasons were given in this newsletter.*]

## Market and Currency Update – 31 March
FTSE 100 – 5,271

Anthony Hilton, the shrewd City editor of the *Evening Standard*, wrote last week that: 'Not only is the international political situation deeply uncertain and dangerous, but stock markets mix heroic valuations with serious uncertainty.'

The 'heroic' valuations persist in two major areas: those of many international blue chips; and those still being placed on a number of leading TMT stocks, such as Vodafone, Reuters, Pearson and Nokia – to my mind still the four most dangerous stocks to hold in terms of potential for further substantial capital loss.

Blue chip valuations refer to solid companies such as those indicated in the following table:

| | Mar 2002 yield | PE | Nov 2010 yield | PE |
|---|---|---|---|---|
| Anheuser-Busch | 1.4% | 23 | 0.84% | 18.5 (now owned by Inbev) |
| Coca-Cola | 1.6% | 26 | 1.7% | 17.7 |
| Kraft Foods | 1.6% | 22 | 3.8% | 15 |
| Colgate Palmolive | 1.2% | 26 | 2.7% | 16 |
| Gillette | 1.9% | 31 | 2.7% | 15 (now owned by Colgate) |
| Nestlé | 1.5% | 25 | 3.5% | 15 |

**Figure 27**

All these companies are financially strong, but in increasingly free world markets intense competition means low future earnings growth, and at these multiples there really must be awfully modest upside.

The problem for general investors is that, if their money is managed by the mainstream big institutions, it is these shares that their portfolios will consist of. Look at the portfolios of any of the big UK managed international investment trusts, and this is what they will be filled with for their US portion, and similar shares for the UK and European portion. On top of that they will still be holding chunks of yesterday's stories – Vodafone, Reuters, Nokia, etc. – which, unless something extraordinary happens, have much further to fall. This is due to the ongoing unravelling of the preposterous excess capacity built up during the boom of 1999/2000.

In these circumstances, investing in these vehicles, or with the big investment houses that mirror such portfolios anyway, looks a sure way of making no money in the foreseeable future.

IT is suffering the worst recession since 1980 due to the concertinaing of capital goods investment before the year 2000 superimposed on the Internet boom, which led to excessive short-term 'panic' investments at overvalued prices in Internet-related products.

So TMT has not turned, but non-TMT looks as if it is in the early stages of a new bull market where performance is already being dominated by the (widely institutionally ignored) low PE sectors of medium and smaller companies almost on a worldwide scale. Meanwhile it has been opined that the outlook for emerging markets is once again bright.

Recently in the emerging markets, the guru of the sector, Angus Tulloch, warned that investors tend to 'move into markets when they have already performed well and are peaking.'

## Market and Currency Update – 1 August
FTSE 100 – 4,202 (close 29 Jul)

[*Between March and September the stock market had suffered a 1,000 point, 20% drop and everybody had become thoroughly unnerved.*]

*Don't panic, Mr Mainwaring*

Working in the stock market in the last month has been like living in a hen coop half occupied by headless chickens and half by instant 'stock market experts'. It is difficult to know which is the lesser of two evils. Basically they are all saying the same thing: that 'capitalism will end by Friday'. Of the two types of inmate, I prefer the headless chickens: at least their behaviour is random.

## BREWIN DOLPHIN SECURITIES

### TMT Index

### UK Market Index ex TMT

**Figures 28 & 29**

James Murray, a retired engineer, who is chairman of the Scottish branch of the UK Shareholders' Association, says: 'You shouldn't sell into falling markets. It is silly unless you think the world is imploding. So why are professionals selling? – unless they know something we don't.'

The answer is they don't. But their world is imploding because it has been built on the assumption that equities always go up, and indeed for the last 25 years to 2000 they always have, with only the briefest of setbacks. Now this glorious certainty, which underpinned the fund management industry, has turned out to have feet of clay.

Think of all the repetitious blabber churned out year after year, persuading the public to buy equities with charts showing their performance against building society deposits, or fixed interest securities. Wonderful lines rising to the sky for equities and a miserable flat line going nowhere for deposits or fixed interest. It was so easy, it was facile.

Now nobody knows what to do. How do you promote equities with a chart over the last three years showing them down by 30%, alongside building society deposits up and likewise for fixed interest?

The FTSE 100 at 4,000, based on the analysts' consensus of 2002 earnings, is now on a PE of 14. This is bang in line with the longer term average. But it hardly constitutes an overshoot on the downward side, which has in the past usually accompanied these cyclical readjustments.

There are, however, some significant straws in the wind:

1. Directors' share purchases have exceeded in the last fortnight by five to one their share sales. This is historically similar to past low points in markets. During the 1998 Russian debt default crisis when the index dipped to 4,400, the ratio of purchases to sales reached nine to one.
2. Technically at 4,000 on the FTSE and 7,800 on the S&P 500, all the leading indices were hugely oversold relative to their 50- day moving averages – by as much as 25%. This was the most oversold technical position we have seen in a decade, and alone suggests the market was overdue for a significant bounce.

[*In October 2002 Morgan Stanley produced a well argued special economic study by Stephen Roach, their chief economist, outlining the risk to the world economy of deflation setting in and a return to the thirties. It was the development of this background of fear during the summer that had sent markets down 1,000 points.*]

## Market and Currency Update – 1 October

According to Ira U. Cobleigh: 'Happiness is a stock that doubles.' The last 12 months are unlikely to have brought her much happiness, but if she is still alive, she might once again have something to smile about in the next 12 months.

Even though the market has approximately halved from its peak (6,900 down to 3,600 last Tuesday), opinions are sharply divided as to where it is going next, with the majority taking the view that worse is still to come. [*This is another example of how in general it is safe to assume that 'the majority' will turn out to be wrong.*]

It might be said therefore that as of today there are two completely rival groups with opposing expectations: the deflationists who currently have the loudest voice; and the cyclicals, or the hopefuls, who see the market implosion as one of the regular cyclical downturns that the economy goes through, and recognise that in due course it will reverse into a resumption of growth.

The deflationists believe that the western economies will now tread the same post-bubble path that has afflicted Japan for the last decade, so that equities may have a long way further to fall, and fixed interest a lot further to rise.

The cyclical school are sceptical of the 1929–1933 revisitation theory, because it has been served up to them at (what with hindsight turned out to be) the 'bottom' or near bottom of every previous stock market crash since the Second World War. In 1998 there was a terrific amount of panic around when Russia defaulted, with fantastic scare stories about major banks going bust. It was the same in 1987, when Wall Street fell 20% in one session; likewise in 1975, when the bottom completely fell out of the market.

Somehow on all three occasions the world managed to get itself going again, and within 12 months markets found a firmer footing, growth resuming, and in the case of the 1975 stock market, it doubled in six weeks.

The only losers in all three cases were those who threw in the towel and sold out at what subsequently turned out to be close to the bottom.

The current charts show very clearly that we are at this critical point now, where we will either go better or break down into a much worse economic scenario. The fixed interest market is at the absolute top of its three-year trading range – exactly the point it reached at the height of the panic of the Russian debt default in September 1998; and every time it has got to this point, it has subsequently fallen back, leaving the 'panic' buyers of fixed interest at those times with quite hefty short-term losses within a few months.

The equity market has now fallen back to the point where the yield of the FTSE All-Share at 3.6% is absolutely in line with its long-term average.

The UK economy is currently stronger, but the extra taxes put in place by Gordon Brown as from next April are exactly the opposite of what should be done to ward off a deflationary threat. Any extra tax burden that immediately deflates profits is deflationary. The return of better profits is the prerequisite for economic recovery and the return of growth.

US economist, Irwin Stelzer, writing in *The Times,* describes the current situation as the American consumer trying to act as the 'heavy locomotive' of the world economy with the headline: 'US loco pulls heavy load of fare dodgers.' In other words, the other nations, in particular Europe, and of course the ever failing Japanese, are doing nothing, or actually the wrong things, to stimulate their consumers.

Europe, with 400 million consumers, more than 12 million unemployed, and plenty of personal savings, along with excessive tax rates, has scope to follow much more aggressive economic policies, by lowering interest rates and making tax cuts. With their Olympian disdain for anything American, the European authorities currently seem deaf to the risks of their inaction.

The other side of the coin is the sheer size of the falls in the European and UK stock markets and of the NASDAQ in the US that have already happened. The risks of difficult economic times ahead definitely appear higher than for the previous cycles, which is probably what the stock market fall is already anticipating, but to conclude from that that the whole economic world is now going to pass through a Japanese style deflation for several years seems more a function of emotional thinking than rational economic assessment.

Those of us who plough through the daily haystack of financial verbiage from so-called financial experts, might be comforted by Michel de Montaigne's words in 1590: 'I prefer the company of peasants because they have not been educated sufficiently to reason incorrectly.'

Likewise, when assaulted at a dinner party by someone claiming that they have a special flair for handling horses, one can remind them of the old Russian proverb on that subject: 'The stupider the peasant, the better the horse understands him' (or her).

## Market and Currency Update – 1 December
FTSE 100 – 4149

I cannot remember a time when a stock market rise (the recent one from the 24 September low of 3,671 to current level) has been so widely described as a 'bear market rally'. The widely held assumption is that it will soon fizzle out.

Meanwhile so-called 'professionals' warn that the market could then fall to new lows. It is worth looking at what the 'professionals' have been advising for the last three years.

In 1998, when the tech sector was stirring strongly, scenting the excitement that lay ahead with the arrival of the Internet, they would not touch tech, on the grounds that it was too expensive and too speculative. In late 1999 when most of these shares had doubled, suddenly the 'professionals' decided that, far from being too expensive, they were now too cheap and piled into them on an unprecedented scale, creating the tech bubble. It was not 'amateur' private investors buying Ericsson at 200 Swedish Krona a share (when the turnover was more than 15 million shares a day, and likewise with Vodafone when it reached 400p); no, this was 95% institutional buying.

To pile Pelium on Ossa they then sold down the shares of solid non-tech businesses, with strong balance sheets, positive cash flow and a good yield, such as Imperial Tobacco (which fell to 330p; now £9.50), Rexam, Reckitt Benckiser, A.B. Foods, and Unilever, etc. And all in order to buy businesses with no yield, no cash flow and no balance sheet!

Having mounted the 'tiger' they then could not get off, and registered horrendous losses in such outfits as Marconi, Cable and Wireless, Energis and Bookham. They then repeated the mistakes in their US and European portfolios.

Now these self-same experts are warning us that the market, after having fallen an unprecedented peacetime 50% (or more in the case of the techs), is set on a new dark age.

Markets are currently discounting the 'fears' of investors, rather than assessing the values of the businesses. Some pretty big investors have caught the 'fear' bug recently, including the venerable Standard Life. It stated in August that it would stick with its high exposure to equities, and then admitted at the end of the quarter that it had sold a cool £4 billion 'to come more into line with its peers'. It is heartening to see that the 'herd' instinct has finally reached our 'woad'-clad colleagues north of Hadrian's Wall.

By contrast, for the last three months we have seen unprecedented director buying, and virtually negligible director selling. The ratio is about 18:1, whereas from January to March 2000 it was nearly 18:1 the other way. Insiders were taking $45 billion a month out of NASDAQ in that period, whilst institutional investors were busily buying up this stock from them – for our pension funds no doubt.

# 9

## *2003*

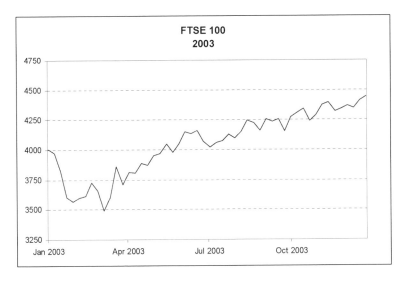

**Figure 30**

*[The recovery in 2003 showed just how important it is to hold one's nerve when everyone is panicking and dark predictions are being made everywhere.]*

## Market and Currency Update – 1 January
FTSE 100 – 3,829 (close 29 Dec)

| Statistics for year to 29 December 2002 | |
| --- | --- |
| FTSE 100 | -27% |
| Europe | -32% |
| Japan Nikkei | -17% |
| Far East | -12% |
| Dow Jones | -16% |
| NASDAQ | -58% |
| Colombia | +24% |

**Figure 31**

*Madness*

I read in a recent edition of *The Sunday Times* that a leading distinguished investment bank has put forward a new scheme whereby landowners can borrow up to 10% of the value of their land – wait for it – to buy hedge funds! The article also suggested that if an investment turned sour, the bank would get the investor out before much money was lost. As many hedge funds do not permit holders to withdraw money without giving three calendar months' notice, and a minimum of one further calendar month, this sounds a dubious assurance.

So far the hedge funds that have imploded, like Long Term Capital Fund, have done so within the period when you cannot sell even if you had had some forewarning.

I have highlighted the danger of these products before, so will not dwell further on them, other than to mention what Barton Biggs, the legendary head of equity strategy at Morgan Stanley, has recently written about hedge funds:

Hedge fund mania that grips the US and Europe has all the characteristics of a classic bubble – it's not as big or as dangerous as the 'tech' bubble, but it could rattle some gilded cages in the financial world. There are now more than 6,000 funds largely unregulated and some highly leveraged.

[*The gilded cages certainly got rattled when the enormity of Bernard Madoff's scam finally came to light with $50 billion losses spread over a very few thousand people.*]

The concept that hedge funds can defy gravity, capturing the upside but with full protection against the downside, is too good to be true. It is difficult to find an instance of anything 'too good to be true' that ever actually happens, other than perhaps an eclipse of the sun.

Extreme concentration of fund management in the UK, due largely to foolish legislation disenfranchising the private investor, and for tax reasons forcing him into the hands of institutions, seems to have resulted in the industry losing its soul. The client used to be close to his advisor; now there is the suspicion that he or she is just part of a sausage machine to produce the fees and commissions for the big fund managers.

The US remains far better served in this respect by its hugely diverse fund management industry, and the competing effect of large numbers of individual investors (almost 50% of the US market is owned by individuals). Furthermore, US investment funds pay capital gains tax, like individuals, so they have no built-in operational benefit.

The charts below (Fig. 32) show what has happened to gold, house prices, gilts (fixed interest securities), and the FTSE 100 in the last 12 months.

The FTSE 100 and virtually all equity investments have suffered grievously, and it is the third year running of falling markets. It is also by far the worst. Last year, for those who had exited the technology sector, it was possible to make

**Figure 32**

good money, as much of the non-tech market – ignored during the tech boom – made a robust recovery. Imperial Tobacco doubled in 2001 along with a number of other old economy shares, and the likes of Shell and Glaxo ended 2001 near all time peaks. Not so this year; virtually the whole market has fallen in a heap, as investors have discovered a new level of panic, throwing out the baby with the bathwater.

It is a characteristic of equity markets that they become the best buy when nobody wants them. The fear of a more prolonged economic downturn is already built into share prices, so the actuality will not be that much of a surprise.

What is not built into share prices is any hope of any better news. Billions of pounds are sitting on the sidelines now.

On top of this there are likely to be very large 'short' positions in markets generally. Everybody talks about what they can see: high debt levels, flagging consumer prospects, profits under pressure, war and terrorist concerns.

Good news does not sell, so the newspapers are full of impending doom. Historically, it is in this kind of emotional situation that the most profitable investments in equities have always been made.

I expect the next major move in stock markets, when it comes, to be upwards, and it will take the market a long way above the current level.

[*Any time during this period subsequently proved to be an excellent time to buy equities.*]

## Market and Currency Update – 1 March
FTSE 100 – 3,570

We are now faced with two markets: the pre-war market and the post-war market. It now looks almost certain that, as a result of the antics of President Chirac, Saddam Hussein (encouraged by this division among the allies) will not disarm unless attacked physically. The French president has brought contempt on himself and humiliation on a great country. It is difficult to find in living memory another example of a head of state who has behaved so waywardly, with the possible exception of, many years ago, President Lumumba of The Congo. He threatened to eat a dissenting member of his Cabinet. Whilst the French president may disdain to coarsen his palate by such an act, he certainly keeps odd company in that part of the world.

As to the peace marches and the 120 Labour MPs who voted against the government, their roots go back directly to those who wanted the British to abandon their nuclear deterrent in the 1950s, and to the pre-war Labour members who voted for total disarmament in the 1930s. (At the time the Labour leader in the Lords, Lord Lansdowne, called for the closure of every army recruiting station in the country in 1928.) This disastrous unpreparedness nearly compromised Britain's own freedom in 1940.

Luckily on this occasion we have courageous leadership, unlike in the thirties when we had no real leaders – just followers of popular public opinion who lacked the courage to warn of the dangers of taking the easy way out. The House of Commons voted three to one in favour of the government's strong stance against Saddam, and even the Labour Party voted two to one in favour.

Al-Qaeda are stateless desperados, who depend for their shelter, training establishments and bases on evil dictatorships, which accept them in return for money or more likely for mafia-style protection. We saw in Taliban-terrorised Afghanistan how they thrived and multiplied. As with mosquitoes, you have to spray the swamps where they breed. Any softening towards a vile regime like Saddam Hussein's merely reinforces such dictatorships everywhere. Regardless of whether Saddam harbours Al-Qaeda, others will.

Latin America was a morass of dictatorships when Galtieri of Argentina overstepped the mark and invaded the Falklands. The same siren voices were heard then advising compromise. But Mrs Thatcher did not flinch, and within six months of Galtieri's defeat nearly every other dictatorship in Latin America was collapsing, and the 'wailing wall' in Argentina had no more missing victims to add to the previous 30,000.

To leave Saddam triumphant will just multiply the hiding places for terrorist activity.

The market in its pre-war mode is at an extreme of nervousness. Investors are staying out because they fear the market may fall further. But stock markets have always been very poor investment guides at their extremes. In 2000 the buoyant market encouraged investors to buy stocks on ludicrous valuations that stood little or no chance of ever being justified.

Now the exact opposite has happened. Now the panic-stricken market is discouraging investors from buying shares when values are so low and dividend yields so high that they offer much better immediate returns than fixed interest, and the prices assume that there will be no growth ever again!

Historically, markets have rallied between 30% and 100% in the first full year after a market hits the bottom. That is when most of the money gets made, and those who know individual companies well, are voting with their feet. Director buying in the UK in the last six months exceeds selling by a ratio of 17:1. The directors scent at least 100%. They believe their company shares have fallen to absurd levels.

## All clear

I believe the share blitz is actually over. There will still be the odd doodlebug that hits a company here or there whose trading turns out to be worse than anticipated. But when we move to the post-war market a debilitating weight will lift from markets. The world post Saddam will actually be a safer place, and the opportunities to start solving some of the Middle East's other perennial problems will be enhanced.

[*The aftermath turned out to be much messier than most of us who were pro knocking out Saddam foresaw. Arguments will rage for years over the decision to invade Iraq.*]

## Broadcasters' bias skews the news (by Dr B. Long)

Sir, I perceive a disease in our broadcasting media. Both radio and television demonstrate a certainty, a unanimity and a superiority that have turned news into views, and comment into the propagation of the one true faith: that of the media editors, reporters and presenters.

The presenters of the news, news background and news review, and even of *Any Questions?, The News Quiz* and *Have I Got News For You,* etc., share a background, education, political stance, personal approach and world view. They are almost all male, white, middle-aged, university educated, left wing, hypercritical, well paid, overbearing, thin skinned and confident in their rightness. They believe that the views of others who hold a different world picture are superficial, biased, intellectually dubious, self-seeking and untenable. These people, no matter what their position, must be interrogated, interrupted, browbeaten, sneered at or made fun of.

Besides the automatic discounting of raw information, there is undisguised contempt for whole areas of world and British news. The Royal family, politicians, George W. Bush and United States figures in general, the established Church, the Conservative Party, the judiciary and we can now add, anything French, must be shown to be ludicrous, self-seeking, unintelligent, remote and unpopular.

The Iraq campaign has been a prime example of the process. The front-men, with no military experience and little hard news, impertinently hector military spokesmen, continually suggest incompetence and insensitivity, question the facts and ridicule the strategy, the logistics, the motives.

These armchair experts do us, themselves and the news a disservice.

Yours faithfully,
B. LONG
23 April, 2003


*Media influence on political perceptions and actions (by Michael Heath)*

Sir, Dr B. Long (letter, April 24) speaks for many of us in denouncing the broadcast media for institutional bias in presenting the news. One could add the none-too-subtle political messages inserted into other programmes such as drama that combine to form a relentless propaganda machine for media-defined political correctness.

There is an interesting contrast here with the printed media that show a much greater diversity of views and achieve a balance thereby. The broadcast media have effectively become a separate political party. They push an agenda with which many disagree profoundly but against which it is almost impossible to find a platform.

For our political life this has enormous implications, one of which is the uphill struggle faced by the Conservative Party in presenting its policies. Radio and television have, with some success, attempted to portray both the party and its supporters as simply risible and not a force to be taken seriously. Even the Labour Party cannot afford to be complacent because, although the views of broadcasters are nearer to its own, Labour has also been slapped down hard when diverging from broadcasters' orthodoxy.

Is it a uniquely British disease, I wonder, to find ourselves subjected to the casual hegemony of media professionals?

Yours faithfully,
MICHAEL HEATH
24 April, 2003

**Market and Currency Update – 1 May**
FTSE 100 – 3,940 (close 28 Apr)

It is believed that the first words of Adam to Eve when they met in the Garden of Eden – somewhere in the rich Euphrates valley (modern Iraq) was: 'Madam, I'm Saddam.' From this portentous first meeting has sprung a string of evil dictators – Genghis Khan, Tamerlane, Suleiman the Magnificent, Hitler, Stalin and Saddam Hussein – who have tried to tear down the civilisations painstakingly built up by the worthier members of mankind. The damage to humanity from these destructive tyrants has varied depending upon the resolution, or lack of it, with which the forces of good at the time have fought against them.

Many French are appalled by the conduct of their president. Corinne Lepage, a former French minister, was given a prime, centre page position in *Le Figaro* for her article against Chirac's leadership headed: 'LA FRANCE DU DESHONNEUR.' In this she stated: 'that more than 30% of the French – an educated cultured people, the nation of the rights of man – dare favour the victory of a bloody tyrant who does not hesitate to use chemical weapons to gas the Kurds, constitutes of our national shame – a complete searching of their consciences is required by the media of the devastating role they have played presenting the news in a totally unbalanced manner, and of which certain televised journalists' clips have been veritable pro-Iraqi propaganda'.

What has all this got to do with the likely evolution of the stock market? Markets are moved by real events, not press prejudice; and the real events of the last month have been astonishingly positive. The sheer speed of the success in Iraq, and the fact that a country of 26 million people and an alleged army of 300,000 can have its regime destroyed by the coalition forces with the loss of under 200 soldiers, points irrevocably to the rottenness of that regime, and the profound fear and hatred with which it was regarded by the vast majority of Iraqis. The media may howl and belittle every peace move because they have so much egg on their face from so wrongly predicting the outcome, but the coalition forces begin the process from a more favourable situation than could have been hoped for at the start of the operations.

The secondary lows of 3,800 on the FTSE and 8,000 on the Dow have held, for the time being, and both indices are breaking out of their 200 days falling moving averages for the first time in three years. War loan, the benchmark of long-

106

dated yields, has three times failed to breach its old peak at 80 (now 74), which would have indicated new high ground for fixed interest (i.e. real deflation or recession).

Only a little fair wind now is needed for a strong change of sentiment and its consequent knock-on effect on economic growth. Should this happen markets will respond very dramatically. Too much money is on the sidelines.

## Market and Currency Update – 1 November
FTSE 100 – 4,303 (close 5 Nov)

*[The significance of this newsletter is the dramatic turn around in the bond market. The triple-A sovereign bond market in 2010 could be just as vulnerable when world economic activity really does pick up.]*

### Markets

Logic suggests that markets should have a setback. Intuition points to a further rise before a correction sets in. Too many people are bullish, which is ominous, but large amounts of cash are still sitting on the sidelines, especially in London and Europe. The charts remain positive. A small amount of good news could quickly bring more of this money onto the table, driving share prices higher quite quickly. Getting the 'feared' rise in interest rates out of the way in the UK could be the catalyst. Paradoxically a rise would be much more positive than another 'hold', which would enhance uncertainty.

Having gorged on excess during the dot-com boom, the market is now terrified of it. So the apparent excesses in the housing market and consumer loans are bad news. An interest rise that was perceived to temper that situation would therefore be good.

## Bonds

Alongside the tremendous recovery in equities since March has been the almost equally dramatic collapse in the fixed interest market, which peaked in June on a ten-year gilt yield of 3.8% and has slumped to 5.03% now. This is one of the biggest reversals seen in a very long time in the fixed interest market, frankly blowing that ten-year 'bull' out of the water. In the short term the reaction looks overdone and appears to be anticipating rises in interest rates that seem unlikely. The other side of the coin is that for the first time for a year it is possible to get a healthy return on cash by investing in bonds. Ten-year gilts yield 5% and medium to good quality industrial bonds yield 6%. Just to confuse the picture further at the very time when quality bonds and government bonds have been slumping, junk or near junk bonds (those of companies with weak balance sheets) have been rising. This is because the perceived worldwide recovery in economic activity makes it much more likely that they will survive; not only that, but they will pay their interest and be redeemed at full face value.

The bond market is therefore signalling a recovery in economic activity and has, for the time being at least, jettisoned the fears of deflation.

Of course both markets could be wrong: the world recovery could stall, and if so, fears of deflation would return, bonds would rocket back up, and junk bonds would collapse along with equities. Modern politics tends, however, to be on the side of equities. 'It's the economy, stupid!' is etched on politicians' hearts and on their seats. Nothing loses elections quicker than deflation, so our democratic system has a built-in propensity to favour stimulative monetary policy.

Central bankers tend to be in the opposite camp, regarding themselves as the defenders of fiscal probity and the value of money, and believing that inflationary stimulation is self-defeating anyway, leading to worse deflation than keeping the money supply under control in the first place. Coming up to elections, politicians tend to press hard on the accelerator, assuming they can reign in the excesses after they have regained power, and if they lose, the opposition inherits the mess anyway.

The best that can be said at the moment is that the rise in equities and the fall in bonds has significantly levelled the playing field of these two opposite asset classes.

## Currencies

Predicting currencies is a very quick way to lose one's reputation, as there is no market that moves more unexpectedly in such a perverse way. Monstrous hedge positions can build up suddenly, amounting to many times the actual volume of transactions needed to finance international trade. 'Cable', the market slang for the US dollar/sterling exchange rate, trades in excess of $100 billion on a normal day. Less than $1 billion would be required to cover the dollar:sterling actual trade transactions in any one day.

We have seen, nevertheless, some fairly significant directional changes in the four leading currencies in the last year. The despised euro has rallied from a low of 0.88 to $US (when Mr Le Pen was shouting his head off) to 1.17 – a 32% rise. Sterling has risen from $1.44 to $1.69 – a 17% change, and the yen, having sat for a long time at the manipulated level of 116 to the dollar, has now 'broken out' to 108 and looks headed at least for parity to the dollar. The Japanese economy does look as if it might at last be freeing itself of its structural strait-jacket, which has constrained that economy for a decade. This, if it is correct, is bullish for the world economy.

The American dollar is feeling the pinch at the cost to the US economy of being the world's policeman. As nobody is willing to share the burden, everybody ends up being forced to, by accepting payment in depreciating dollars for their wares. Who is going to rock the boat? The Far East certainly won't, and the Europeans certainly would be unhappy to see the euro rise a lot further, so one suspects this is how the world will continue to pay for managing its security threat. Only the French resent it, and might risk seeing the whole pack of cards collapse to humiliate the Americans. But under Chirac their credibility has plummeted, and they are increasingly isolated.

Currency trends when they change tend to go on for longer than the underlying economic situation justifies. The euro fell too far relative to the underlying strength of the European balance sheet before its 30% plus rally. The dollar too may fall too far before it rallies, but at its present level, any visitor to the US will appreciate what good value it already is.

# 10

## *2004*

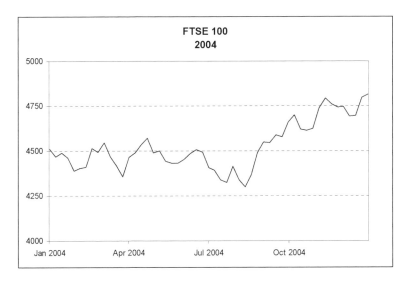

**Figure 33**

## Market and Currency Update – 28 January
FTSE 100 – 4,447

One of the most dependable ways of losing money over the years has been accepting advice to diversify into the 'new trend'.

111

It is the unfortunate feature of financial services that almost all products are sold on past performance (usually just at the point that that performance is about to expire) rather than future prospects. Or rather the implication is that future prospects will continue past performance. From 1966 – the peak of the first post-war equity boom – through to 1980, equities performed very poorly, showing no overall (inflation-adjusted) gain, other than for the rare few who had bought during the market's collapse in 1974/5. The new trend was to diversify into agricultural land, then approaching the equivalent in today's prices of £4,600 an acre (in 1982).

Jim Slater (former Chairman and founder of Slater Walker and iconic investment guru) had given the advice: 'Buy, until you reach the sea' and 'They are not making it any more.' Every leading pension fund and insurance company in the country had plunged in, no doubt egged on by their actuaries, and bought tracts of the UK at these heady levels. Twenty years later the last of those purchases have finally been dumped at less than £2,300 an acre, the current price. [*Agricultural land started to rise again from 2005 onwards and today sells at between £5,000 and £7,000 an acre just after they finished selling.*]

Equities of course were being shunned in 1982, which turned out to be the beginning of the biggest bull market that century, showing a compound return of more than 17% annually for the next 20 years.

The next fashionable new trend to come along was in 1994, five years after the Berlin Wall had come down. This was the 'emerging markets' boom. In that year no less than 80 new funds were launched to accommodate the fever for emerging market exposure. As the quoted securities in these markets were few and very small, the avalanche of cash from Western institutions quickly pushed valuations to ridiculous heights. This was a classic case of: 'there is no asset class that cannot be spoiled by too much money.' Luckily the total did not amount to more than 2–5% of equity portfolios, so when the Asian crisis of 1996 engulfed the sector and sent PEs reeling from over 20 to below 5, sending some markets down 80%, the damage overall was small.

But a 'one-way' ticket for equities (they could only go up) was gathering some serious momentum after 15 years of rising markets, and when the next 'trend' appeared – the Internet and the new tech boom – institutions were not just going to risk 5% of their money as with the emerging markets trend, or the agricultural one. This time it was 'the big one'.

Anything up to 25–30% of portfolios were switched into TMT; and at the prices stocks were pushed up to, TMT turned into TNT! When the gelignite did explode it blew a massive hole in worldwide equity portfolios – worse in London than New York. The quality of London fund management fell to a level of passive, sheep-like index shadowing, benchmark hugging and suspension of judgement that left the City's reputation in tatters.

One small flame of individuality and independent thinking was kept alive by ED & F Man. The leadership there saw that the 29-year bull market must be close to its death, if for no other reason than by excessive overvaluation, and launched a series of funds designed to benefit from falling markets, or that avoided equities.

Fortune smiled on the brave, as it turned out to be the longest and deepest bear market for 30 years. So for three years in a row, the essentially 'short' funds pioneered in London by Man flourished, and spawned a veritable industry of 'hedge' funds, as many lesser lights clambered on that bandwagon. Some were admittedly good fund managers, who could not tolerate any longer the myopic parameters within which they had been forced to work by the big fund management groups.

But now there are more than 7,000 so-called hedge funds, mostly offshore and unregulated; in other words a casino – a vast battery of slot machines. You take your choice and pay a hefty up-front fee for the privilege, but very few will produce the 'silver cadillac'.

But it is a bandwagon because essentially the thinking behind hedge funds is 'short', not 'long', and they were bound to seriously underperform once the market turned. Hence last year the six leading hedge funds averaged a mere 3% appreciation, whilst stock markets in general rose between 15% and 50%.

Most people joined the hedge fund craze just at the moment when they stopped performing, and to do so, got out of equities just at the moment when they started performing.

2003 has been one of the best years in stock market history, with huge gains in all secondary markets and medium capitalisation. The Far East is up nearly 50% with Thailand over 100% and India 90%. Virtually all those markets have had a tremendous run, except the Philippines. Latin American markets have boomed with Brazil having trebled from the low hit when the new left-wing president was elected, and panic reigned.

Russia doubled, but now looks as if it is on the way back down again as President Putin goes in to strip the ill-gotten gains off the oligarchs. The Dow-Jones is now only 7% off its all time peak. The NASDAQ is still 50% below the bubble level, but has recovered more than 100% from its low, and by historical standards PEs of the technology stocks are back to the very top of their range (20 x to 35 x over 30 years ignoring the 80 x of the bubble).

Money and liquidity remain plentiful. The falling dollar is shifting the imbalances of the US economy onto the rest of the world, as America wisely never borrows in anything but the currency of which it controls the printing press! And that press has been on overtime recently. But now the risks of deflation seem to have been significantly reduced, this process is likely to stop, and that could pose a real threat to currently

114

**CONVERTIBLES**

# Scandal fall-out hits hedge funds

By Elizabeth Rigby in London

The fall-out from the crisis engulfing Parmalat and its creditors has seen a number of European hedge funds suffer losses during December.

Goldman Sachs' European convertible arbitrage index showed that hedge funds using this strategy were down on average 2.1 per cent during the month with some funds posting losses of more than 6 per cent.

Barep Asset Management, a unit of Société Générale's asset management arm, was particularly hard hit. Its €330m convertible arbitrage fund lost about 7 per cent in December, according to market sources. The fund ended the year down 3.5 per cent.

A convertible arbitrage fund typically buys up a company's convertible bonds and shorts the shares. The aim is to profit from pricing anomalies between convertible bonds and the company's underlying stock.

Parmalat, which in September disclosed it had released €1.2bn in convertible bonds across four different issues, was an obvious play. But many investors were caught out by the rapid drop in the value of Parmalat's convertibles since the beginning of December.

The sell-off started at the end of November when Parmalat missed its self-imposed deadline to recoup €496.5m it said was placed in Epicurum, a Cayman Islands investment fund whose existence has been questioned by investigators.

Market jitters were exacerbated in December when the dairy group narrowly missed defaulting on a bond repayment after Italian banks and the Italian government stepped in. Hedge fund managers and bankers estimated that 80-90 per cent of the value of the convertibles has been wiped out.

"It has been very painful for some people out there," said one hedge fund manager. "Many hedge funds would have held credit default swaps, which helped, but the magnitude of the event and the speed with which things unfolded conspired to make full hedging an impossibility."

KBC, the Belgian bank, which runs $3.3bn across five different hedge funds, said its two funds with significant exposure to Parmalat had had a difficult December.

Its $800m Convertible Opportunities Fund was off 0.47 per cent, ending the year up 16.85 per cent, while its $600m Credit Arbitrage Fund was up 0.67 per cent for the month and 14.25 per cent for the year.

Andy Preston, managing director of KBC Alternative Investment, said: "Apparent misrepresentations of balance sheet on such a massive scale are rare, but will continue to happen. Though we can never fully protect ourselves from all eventualities, through solid risk management and portfolio diversification, we can emerge from these events relatively unscathed."

**Figure 34**

115

stretched asset values. We may now be back in a bull market, but a shake-out does look more than due.

## Market and Currency Update – 1 March
FTSE 100 – 4,522 (close 23 Feb)

Many of us in investment management have been on record for some time in the view that if an edict could be pronounced abolishing the Mergers and Acquisitions departments of the world's leading investment banks, capitalism would be substantially richer today than it is.

There appears to be a systemic weakness in the current capitalist system that enables the managers of big companies to embark on ego trips of acquisition expansion, which also hugely benefit the bankers that advise them and far too often end up in massive destruction of shareholder value.

According to a study by KPMG, over the last ten years 70% of these deals have lost significant value. In some cases they have even led to the obliteration of the company, as in the case of Marconi. So much so that the highly regarded fund management company, Franklin Templeton, as a matter of principle, has for some years sold shares in any company it holds that embarks on an acquisition spree. It does not wait for the outcome, as historically the odds have been so dramatically against that outcome being successful.

The greatest companies in the world have almost all been built through organic growth. However, nothing works in the end better than letting free market forces sort out the market's own problems, rather than reverting, as in EU style, to rigid legislation; and we are now seeing an important shareholder backlash to this record of failure. Again, so much so that the stock market enjoyed its single best day for three months on the day that Vodafone had to announce that its bid for AT&T Wireless had failed. However, this was not such good news for shareholders in Vodafone who find themselves with a CEO who is already 'damaged goods' only a few months into his stewardship.

Nevertheless, this is very good news for shareholders generally. The formerly distorted balance of power between the boardroom and the owners of the businesses is being redressed, and we should see much better thought out corporate activity than in the past, where all too often the principal motivation was the managers' desire to be king of a bigger castle, regardless of whether its foundations were built on rock or sand (usually the latter).

This brings me on – for the final time – to the most unfortunate pendulum effect still infecting investors as a result of the equity losses most of them endured in the big bear market of 2000–2003: the lurch into hedge funds.

Firstly, 90% of these devices are offshore and therefore unregulated. Investors do not appreciate that they may have to give up to one month's notice to quit, and the value date could be a minimum of 30 days after the order is given; furthermore, payment might then be up to as much as 60 days after that.

As a private client broker these products come to me from time to time with new portfolios to manage, for example, in June 2002 a hedge fund from the GAM management group came with a portfolio from a leading UK bank. I gave the instruction to sell in early June. I was informed that the valuation date would be 30 July, and payment 30 September. The client was totally unaware that she had been locked in, in this way, by her bank 'relationship' manager.

## Market and Currency Update – 1 June
FTSE 100 – 4,422 (close 2 Jun)

Recently, Shell has been accused of exaggerating its statutory reserves and fined for allegedly misleading investors. An interesting letter from the CEO of Glasgow Investment Managers was recently printed in the *Financial Times* about this issue, as follows:

> Sir,
> Over the past 30 years Shell's share price and dividend in the UK have risen by about twice as much as the FTSE All-Share index, the representative index of UK share price performance, and the average dividend on UK companies' shares. One can only wish that the fund management industry, or the government, had done as well.
>
> So will the regulators, commentators, corporate governance experts, and fund managers, please let the management of Shell get on with the job it does very well professionally, and allow it to employ the governance structure it considers appropriate. Talk is cheap, because there is a lot of it about, and all it does is divert management from its proper task.

Quite. And the interesting stock market lesson is: Follow the 'popular wisdom' in the press at your financial peril. Shell has been the second best performing FTSE 100 stock since this supposed scandal broke when the shares were marked down to 370p, bottoming at 350p a few days later.

The storm in a teacup so splendidly blown up by the media and then the FSA, belatedly sticking in its oar, created a superb buying opportunity.

This brings me to the present state of the stock market

where I seem to find myself in agreement with the 'general feeling', which means I am almost certainly losing my touch! (The majority view is usually wrong.) At the moment the majority view seems to be:

1. Pessimism about equities due to rising oil prices and the general fear that they will stay higher for longer than seemed likely a month ago.
2. That the Iraq aftermath is going so badly that it is now diminishing economic confidence. This, combined with permanently higher oil prices, means lower than expected world growth in the next 12 months, feeding quickly through to less robust profit revival.

As these concerns are widely held they are almost certainly priced in, so one should in fact be buying. This is because (A) there is a huge 'bull' position in oil futures, which will unravel at some point, leading anyway to a short-term relapse in oil prices; and (B) the worst in Iraq is probably in the past, and better news may start to flow from there. Furthermore, the rise in fuel prices has not yet been enough to unhinge the fairly strong upward trend of world growth.

However, the caveat that does concern me is the historical: No other markets ever manage to defy completely the gravity 'pull' of whatever the US market is doing.

With so much caution around in the London market at the moment and much less demanding PEs than Wall Street, the short-term situation is more robust. But the wider picture, with too much debt creation generally in the Anglo-Saxon economies, is not compelling for equities at current levels.

[*Looking back on this newsletter, its conclusions about the market levels and the high price earnings along with the ratio of market capitalisation to GDP were right technically – an unsustainable valuation situation was already quite advanced.*

*It was at this point that the Fed (with hindsight) seemed to go wrong. Debt accumulation in the US was already dangerous for stability, and stock prices were already in too high ground to be sensible. Instead of tightening hard and immediately, this situation continued with a loose monetary policy for another two years. That, and the covert creation of even more liquidity through the development of shadow banking and derivative market operations, sent markets up nearly another 50% by the end of 2007 and created trillions more debt. This then laid the foundations for the subsequent massive financial crash.]*


## Market and Currency Update – 1 July
FTSE 100 – 4,531 (28 Jun)

It now appears fairly evident that the world's leading central bankers had a nasty shock about 18 months ago. That is except Wim Duisenberg, the EU's chosen central banker. The same could be said of him as was said of President Coolidge by his personal aide. The latter rushed out of the president's bedroom in the White House one morning and wailed:

'The president is dead.'

'How can you tell?' said the vice president.

So with the exception of Duisenberg all the central bankers thought they might be faced with a possible spiral of deflation, resulting from the fall-out of the dot-com burst bubble back in 2001. Shades of the 1930s started to loom before their eyes. Led by Alan Greenspan (Chairman of the Federal Reserve), they embarked on one of the most impressive monetary reflations ever seen by man.

In the short term this has certainly had the beneficial effect of shunting potential deflation into the sidings, but we are left with an awesome aftermath of excess liquidity, which has leaked out into assets all over the place.

Meanwhile the highly respected head of PIMCO and

120

creator of the world's largest bond fund, Bill Gross, a man with an incredible record of achieving something of the order of 9% compound growth from his fund over more than 20 years, says he believes the right price for the Dow is 5,000 (it was Greenspan who warned of 'irrational exuberance' when the Dow reached 6,800!). He also believes that 'bonds have had their day'. That latter remark was made before bond markets had endured their recent substantial sell-off. He also said he had taken the maximum permissible amount of his fund (20%) out of dollars and placed it in sterling and euro bonds. Hardly a resounding ring of confidence in the dollar.

The problem facing the dollar is that three years have now elapsed without even a minor tilt by the authorities to address the considerable imbalances – both in international trade and domestic over-borrowing. Greenspan has acquired such an aura of walking on water that people might believe his magical powers will somehow make the problem go away. [*We should all have been more mindful of what President Nixon's economic advisor, Herb Stein, had once said: 'If something cannot go on for ever, it will stop.'*]

There are a lot of big forces out there to prevent a dollar rout, which the doomsters, the gold bugs (mainly living in nuclear bunkers round Lake Zurich) and hedge fund 'short' merchants keep predicting – or rather talking up the position they have already taken in the market.

The dollar plainly became heavily oversold when it hit 1.90 to the pound back in March, then rallied to 1.76 mainly on short covering; and now that rally, not sustained by any improvement in the fundamentals, seems to have petered out, and the slide seems to be resuming. How far is difficult to say. The figure of 1.90 is a tough hurdle to pass (we were there back in 1991), but it could sink back there especially if Greenspan is 'measured' in his manifest lateness to move interest rates up in the US.

All this makes world stock markets a very tricky place at

the moment in which to make money. In the words of Philip Coggan of the *Financial Times* column the 'Long View', one should be 'cautious of the extent to which current economic growth has been "borrowed" from the future thanks to low interest rates and loose fiscal policy'.

## Market and Currency Update – 1 November
FTSE 100 – 4,621

*Investment planning advice*

Mark Tinker is a certified (he was recently certified by his doctor and he has just been 'authorised' by the FSA) financial planner at Platinum Investments advisors, and he has been asked by Mr and Mrs Gene Sucker, a recently retired couple, to advise them on what to do with their 'Lazy' lump sum, as the recent advert from The Pru puts it. The Suckers have about £240,000 of cash in the bank, a £40,000 lock-up garage in Chelsea and a time share on the Costa Lotta (bought for £20,000 in the eighties 'time share boom' but now worth £2,000, and costing £3,000 a year in maintenance). They also have a home in London worth £1.5 million; it is a semi-detached broom cupboard close to Harrods.

They intend to sell the house and move to a smaller one in the same neighbourhood (perhaps a disused telephone box), and they want to invest the proceeds so that they can go on regular cruises, which they have dreamed of, and live comfortably in the years of retirement ahead of them. Gene says, 'The performance of the stock market over the last five years makes us very wary of committing any of our eventual funds in this way.' Therefore, they are looking for alternative investments.

Mark Tinker took them down to the Alternative Investment Show at Canary Wharf, where the first stand they came to was that of Stanley Gibbons. The salesman there proudly told them that over the last five years a 'good' portfolio of stamps had actually nearly doubled in value. So with Mark's agreement, they gave Stanley Gibbons a cheque for £100,000 to invest on their behalf in a collection of stamps.

The next stand was, if anything, even more interesting. It was an EIS scheme (Enterprise Investment Scheme) to farm cod, which, thanks to our European Union partners, have been dredged out of the North Sea, so are now in extremely short supply. Also the Chancellor's generosity meant that they could get 40% tax relief on the first £100,000 they put into this scheme. So they plunged a net £60,000 into cod, giving them a notional interest in the company of £100,000.

Next they went to a stand called The Hedged Fund of Hedge Funds. The (slick) presentation here claimed that whatever markets did, whether they went up, down or side-ways, or did cartwheels, their sophisticated hedging of hedging, meant that they couldn't lose (that is of course excluding the 4% up-front fee, and the 2% annual fees, and, oh yes, they were locked in for five years). So they made a mental note that when the house was sold this fund would be an obvious receptacle for a good chunk of the proceeds.

Five years on: Sadly things have not worked out quite as well as the Suckers had hoped. They put their home on the market for £1.5 million. But apparently that had been a valuation around the top of the market in 2003, and nobody came up with an offer anywhere near that. Meanwhile they had downsized to a £1 million house, which they bought with a bridging loan from their all too obliging bank, which of course had the security of their £240,000 current account balance, and the old house, and the new house. But bridging loans don't come cheap, and theirs was charged at a hefty 8%. After three years of getting no offers at £1.5 million, and with mounting pressure on them from the bank manager, they finally accepted an offer of a round £1 million. This repaid the bridging loan, but the original £240,000 in their current account had now passed into the hands of the bank, which had taken out £80,000 a year for the three years in interest charges.

The Stanley Gibbons stamps had not done too badly; the kindly manager at Stanley Gibbons said he thought he could get about the same price they had paid for the collection five years ago, but they should realise when they had bought, stamps were a very popular alternative investment and the prices had been (with the benefit of hindsight) rather too high then.

As for the cod farm enterprise, this had apparently gone very well for the first two years; then a disease (from over-stocking apparently) had swept through the cod, killing about one third of them. It would have been all right, except that Health & Safety had then put in the boot by insisting the rest of the stock must be destroyed as they could 'possibly' be a public health hazard. So, alas, this tax efficient investment had indeed been tax efficient, but there was still nothing left of it.

To rub salt in the wound, the £40,000 lock-up garage – no longer any use to them as they could not now afford a car – was being rented for £3,000 a year to house the new BMW of their former financial advisor.

They sensibly sold the time share and got £2,000, so at least that was a success, and they have no outlays any more on that.

Their dream of spending much of their retirement cruising on the high seas has not entirely gone by the board, funnily enough, although it has taken a slightly unexpected form.

Gene Sucker has got a job as a steward on the SS *Oriana*, a plush P&O cruise ship, and his wife is employed in the kitchens cutting vegetables for one of the under chefs. They share a small steerage cabin – unfortunately with limited views, as it is below the waterline – but when the ship lists badly, they do get an occasional glimpse of the horizon.

Says Gene: 'One thing I have learnt from this experience is that the only piece of information on a financial product you can truly ever rely on to turn out to be accurate is the standard statement: "Past performance is no guarantee of future performance." '

He also says that the one sector he avoided at the time because of 'poor past performance' was the stock market. Unfortunately for Gene, over the subsequent five years it rose a solid 40%, and would have given a rising income from increased dividends starting at 4.5% on the money and reaching 6% today.

That said, he felt he had been lucky in the end because he had had no money left to put into the Hedged Fund of Hedge Funds. When he rang the overseas number to find out how they had done, he just got a blank ringing tone: line disconnected.

## *The stock market*

Currently there is a wide range of contradictory strands leading to a confusing economic outlook. Many of these will be affected by the outcome of the US presidential election. Next month, after that uncertainty is out of the way, an attempt will be made to see whether there is a pattern emerging from the many contradictory signals.

| Principal capital indices for six months to 5 October: | | | |
|---|---|---|---|
| FTSE 100: | +5.05% | FTSE All-Share | +4.54% |
| FTSE world | +0.98% | Dow-Jones | −1.77% |
| Tokyo Topix | −8.28% | FTSE Asia Pacific ex Japan | +0.58% |

**Figure 35**

## Market and Currency Update – 1 December
FTSE 100 – 4,760 (22 Nov)

'If the trumpet gives an uncertain sound who will answer the call?' Alexander Pope

[*At the time of writing this newsletter, President George W. Bush had just won a second term, much to the disgust of most of Europe.*]

President Bush, for one, hasn't suffered from this particular problem. His trumpet was loud and clear, and it was answered unequivocally this time. He did not have to win Florida with the help of 20,000 lawyers. As a consequence, Europe has gone into a sulk; the loftier the intellect, it seems, the bigger the sulk. But forget not the words of Lord Melbourne: 'What all the wise men said would happen has not happened, and what all the damn fools predicted has occurred.'

But interestingly the first person to snap out of the sulk was our old king of spin himself, Alastair Campbell. The next day he wrote an article in *The Times,* pointing out the futility of such a stance, and remonstrating that only Europe would suffer if the UK did not co-operate with a clearly re-empowered George Bush.

Now that the massively reasonable (and indeed reasonably massive) Colin Powell has stepped off the hurtling right-winged only spacecraft, an even greater swallowing of prejudice will be needed by European leaders if they want to have any influence on Bush at all.

The political consequences of his victory might actually turn out rather better than the viscerally anti-American Europeans fear, but we are primarily concerned with the economic consequences and these must be good.

The Bush team will handle the US's economic problems much better than Kerry, because their core strategy of enhancing the wealth-creating sector with tax cuts, and not adding to the wealth-consuming public sector, is the rubber stamp of successful economies.

For two months I have ducked the big question of the conflicting economic runes, and the famous Twin Deficits (the systemic balance of payments deficit and the Federal budget deficit both running at about -6% of GDP) of the US economy, which now rank in stock market folklore almost as large as the Twin Towers of 9/11.

Bush's victory removes one uncertainty, and markets obviously liked that, but with the S&P 500 standing on a PE of 21.25 x there is plenty of room for disappointment. Of course no past major bear market has ever ended on a PE anything like as high as 21 x. Yet within the market there are extraordinary differences. For example, oil majors are on a modest PE of about 12; and the top five Internet stocks – Google, Yahoo, eBay, Amazon and Yahoo Japan share an average PE of 80.

The big figure, however, is that the combined market cap of the US-quoted economy currently represents 54% of the MSCI world index – a figure impossible to equate with the actual size of the US economy relative to the world. This is reminiscent of when Japan's share of the MSCI in its 1990 bubble rose to 37% (it is now barely 10%).

Steven Roach, the investment guru of Morgan Stanley, believes that the twin deficits have now piled up to so great a level, and with no sign in sight of any effort by the administration to tackle them, that an inflexion point has been passed. [*He was right and we should have listened to him more attentively*.] The inevitable result of this will be a collapse of the dollar, and a world economic crisis.

Of more concern are the words of Austrian-American economist and political scientist, Joseph Schumpeter, who once said:

For any revival which is due mainly to artificial stimulus leaves part of the work of depressions undone and adds, to an undigested remnant of maladjusted, more maladjustments of its own.

Alan Greenspan is beginning to tighten. Unlike Paul Volcker before him, he may, indeed he already has, lagged behind the inflationary curve. As the credit screws gradually tighten, US savings will rise, and domestic consumption will fall. [*This alas did not happen.*] The fall will hit imports much faster than domestic industry, because of the very high proportion of consumer goods imported. Walmart alone imported $15 billion from China last year.

What will happen to the current massive 'shorts' of the dollar when its trade balance begins to improve? A second recession seems inevitable to complete the work of the first, but the Fed will do its best to make it saucer-shaped like last time, rather than V-shaped.

In terms of Wall Street this all means that corporate profits will be taking a dip in some but not all areas of the US economy in the fairly near future; and overall the current S&P valuation of 21 x cannot possibly absorb that.

[*Already those with good foresight were drawing attention to the unsustainable nature of America's twin deficits; among them, Barton Biggs was clearly warning that the US was heading for a fall. We now know it was prolonged by two things:*

1. *China's keenness to vendor finance the USA's excessive Chinese imports, thus keeping the pressure off the dollar, which would have happened if they had been unwilling to pile up ever larger dollar balances.*
2. *Greenspan's far too dilatory tightening of monetary policy in the US. This was partly encouraged by the*

*cushion to inflation supplied by (1), but it was also partly because Greenspan lacked the skill of Volcker.*

*Andrew Smithers, a distinguished economist who operates his own economic think tank in London, throughout this period was also drawing attention to the complete non-sustainability of the ever rising US debt.*

*I was already becoming concerned that markets were being fuelled by excess liquidity, and that much of the underlying earnings growth was being created by very unsustainable consumer expenditure, resulting from increased personal borrowing. The new syndrome of people using the collateral of their homes (in the USA and the UK) as an ATM machine was also clearly a bogus form of economic stimulation.*

*In theory, markets should have begun to retrench – in fact they had another two years of boom ahead; a boom founded on rising debt rather than wealth creation.*

*This was going to make the eventual day of reckoning much worse. How much worse we could not possibly guess because nobody at that point was talking about the possibility of an international banking crash superimposing on the inevitable cyclical recession due to come sooner or later.]*

## Market and Currency Update – 22 December
FTSE 100 – 4,725 (close 21 Dec)

The Prudential last month sold its freehold of Burlington Arcade for £65 million. This has always been a prime piece of real estate in London but has been altered very little since they bought it in 1955 for £265,000.

The West End now has the highest rental rates in the world, and the City the second highest, which it certainly did not have in 1955. So some appreciation is due to the one-off effect of London becoming a magnet for the world's wealthy, the Hong Kong of Europe, and arguably the most successful capital city (at the moment) on the globe. But also much of the monetary increase is due to the collapse of the purchasing power of printed paper money (£s) since 1955.

In the nineteenth century when the pound was pegged to gold it held its purchasing power more or less for 100 years. This scenario will never return so long as the discipline of the printing presses is in the hands of politicians.

A useful statement was made last week by the top strategic team at Morgan Stanley on the dollar. Referring to the rebalancing that has to take place, and that Greenspan has now given official notice of, they say: 'Yet everyone is insisting it won't hurt.'

This looks to be a universal error of judgement. It is almost inconceivable that this rebalancing can take place without some 'hurt' somewhere. Stock markets generally are at 12-month highs, or all time highs (Latin America, Australia, India). They are simply not factoring in this risk.

China may revalue somewhat, and most of the other Far Eastern currencies also. This would represent the biggest aid to the rebalancing, and it looks as if this is already beginning to happen, though at a glacial pace.

Europe still appears very negative, reluctant to tackle the welfare and public sector drag on its economies – call it Euro-bloatism. [*One has to nevertheless admit that Euro-bloatism has produced for Europeans some of the best infrastructure, in the form of roads, railways, health care and schooling, anywhere in the world today, including America (though probably not as good as Japan).*]

Much depends on whether politicians will continue to thwart market forces for fear of losing the votes of those (with vested interests) that change will hurt. It is worth quoting Carlo Capello:

All empires seem to eventually develop an intractable resistance to change needed for the required growth of production. Then neither the needed enterprise nor the needed type of investment, nor the needed technology change is forthcoming.

David Schwartz, a well reputed stock market historian, states:

The painful message is that lengthy [stock market] advances are typically followed by protracted periods of disappointment, regardless of inflation, politics, economic cycles, war, peace, or even the century one chooses to analyse.

# 11

## *2005*

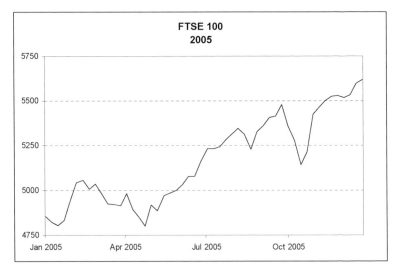

**FTSE 100
2005**

**Figure 36**

*[The year 2005 was to turn out to be a good one for equities; the FTSE 100 rose 10.7% from 4,850 to 5,625. But the star performers were commodities and emerging markets, which rose in the region of 30%, and investors started to get enraptured by the idea of a super cycle in commodities. Emerging markets, which in general earned the bulk of their wealth from*

132

*commodity sources, consequently followed close behind. Property shares in the UK also had a very good year.*]

## Market and Currency Update – 1 March
FTSE 100 – 5,015

PRICE, PRICE, PRICE and PATIENCE. These are the core ingredients for profitable investment. If you pay too much, you have merely created the profit for the person you bought from.

The very nature of stock markets is that they have a dangerous suction effect on unwary investors. Markets rise when people don't expect them to, and after it has happened people see the profits that others have made, and want to get in on the action; consequently they are sucked in just as the game is ending.

In a brokerage office one sees this perhaps more obviously than in other investment institutions. Towards the top of every stock market cycle (and the rise from 3,287 in March 2003 to 5,000 plus today is one such cycle) calls start coming in asking for ideas or worse still – a good spec! Suddenly people find they have got some spare money. They had it all the time, they just did not want to buy when markets were cheap but looked scary; and the newspapers, as always, were telling them to steer clear when they should have been buying.

Now of course they are talking of blue sky and it is safe to buy. What rot! If the price is wrong it is not safe to buy, and a lot of prices are now fully reflecting the potential. Far too often everyone forgets that stock markets are first and foremost discount mechanisms rather than accurate measurers of value. By and large everything that is in the news is already discounted in the price. Profit only comes when market perception of a stock or a sector is lower than the outcome. By definition, this means buying into shares or sectors that are not in fashion, because in their case, market perception is probably below their realistic prospects.

Bubbles happen all the time, and there are quite a few in the making at the moment. Mining and oil exploration stocks top the list, and a lot of emerging markets – Turkey, India, Latin America – are rising like Icarus towards the sun. They may have further to go, but it is 'tiger riding' and tigers are not easy to dismount.

Chartists have been warning for over a year that if the London market got to 5,000 this would represent a massive hurdle to overcome. Until the latest rise in worldwide indices, equities represented much the best value for money around as an asset class. This is now somewhat more debatable at the current level.

There is another problem with very large companies that may militate against their performance. It is the systemic tendency of large organisations to become bureaucratic. They consequently lose their dynamism, and in some cases drive out the more entrepreneurial spirits, who find it difficult to work in that kind of culture.

Few so far in the investment world have appreciated the trend-breaking decision of Lord Hanson to cut the old Hanson Group into four separate companies. He saw the group was getting too large for its own good. The result has been a spectacular creation of shareholder value. By contrast, so many companies that have made themselves even larger through big acquisitions have spectacularly destroyed shareholder value in the process – only a few need to be mentioned: Marconi, Vivendi Universal, Cable and Wireless, Daimler-Benz (with the Chrysler acquisition) and so on.

The decision of Procter & Gamble to join with Gillette looks perverse. It might have been better for shareholders if each company had split itself into smaller units rather than become one mighty juggernaut.

To bring together these various strands in conclusion:

Firstly, we see that disgust with stock market losses in 2002/2003 has led to a flight from stocks into property, accentuated somewhat in the UK by the stiffer solvency requirements imposed on life companies by new regulation. The flow of money into commercial property has pushed yields down to very low levels, which now offer disappointing medium-term returns in this asset class.

Secondly, whilst the stock markets of most of the world have now made a very good recovery from the dark days of March 2003 when the FTSE 100 fell to 3,283, the weight of money that has moved elsewhere suggests that as an asset class they are not in general suffering from inflated values due to excess flows of capital; if anything, the reverse. But they currently look like being at the top end of a short-term cycle.

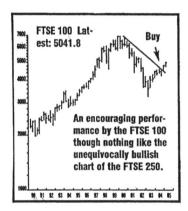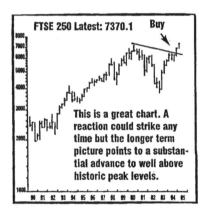

Figure 37

## Market and Currency Update – 31 March
FTSE 100 – 4,910 (29 Mar)

*The property market*

A false situation has undoubtedly developed in the commercial property asset market, which is well recognised by the professionals, but does not seem to have been by investors.

Last year commercial property was the best performing asset class, returning 18.7%; on top of this, property shares rose 48%. Land Securities is now just under double its price of two years ago, largely eliminating the traditional discount at which property shares trade.

But the anomaly is that rising asset values have not been underpinned by rising rentals. A one-off enforced shift of investment assets from equities into property by the big savings institutions – life companies and pension funds – is the likely cause.

The result is that yields in the property market on good covenants have fallen to such low levels that many big commercial holders of property, such as hotels, supermarkets etc., have been selling their properties and leasing them back. The list is impressive: Intercontinental, Tesco, Somerfield, Debenhams, Boots and Royal Bank of Scotland.

When professionals get out on this scale, investors should be wary of the inflated values they are currently enjoying on their property shares.

## Market and Currency Update –1 May
FTSE 100 – 4,792

*'Sorry, we haven't any money left!'*

The excellent financial team at *The Times,* headed by Patience Wheatcroft, yesterday published its economic commentary under the above banner.

What has happened is that Gordon Brown's damaging stewardship of the UK economy in Labour's second term – the first was quite good – has now killed the growth of wealth therein, after having artificially puffed up consumer expenditure for four years. This was brought about because of two main factors:

1.  Brown managed to convert a government surplus of £30 billion into a deficit of the same order, i.e. pumping an extra £60 billion credit into the economy almost annually. As Warren Buffet says: 'Give me a billion dollars and I will show you consumer growth.'
2.  This, along with a previous structural shortage, has increased house prices in the UK by 78% in the lifetime of this government, leading to a further one-off, but unrepeatable 'equity withdrawal' from the underlying surge in the temporary value of people's homes. Mortgage lending has risen from £600 billion to £1,000 billion in the last four years, of which it is estimated that only £200 billion was used to finance the new stock of houses built, and the rest has swelled the consumer boom. A good illustration is the rise in spending in the UK on DIY from £11 billion to over £14 billion since 2001.

A combination of higher interest rates and the £70 billion extra tax take has finally drained people of any extra spending money. House prices have stopped rising so equity withdrawal has largely ceased.

But for the first time for a decade net UK earnings have fallen this year, as this chancellor has over-raided the productive sector of the economy, and shifted the money into the state sector where most of it has gone up in smoke.

The American consumer has shared with the British the

same artificially boosted consumer boom on the back of rising house prices. A burgeoning government fiscal deficit is financing today's consumer expenditure from tomorrow's savings. It is inevitable that the US consumer will slow down now. Wall Street is probably telling us this anyway; it is down 6% from the start of the year and does not appear to have finished falling yet.

To get back to the chronic US trade and budgetary imbalances, all of these are inside the dollar block, the excessive US deficits being fully covered by the equally excessive savings of the others: China and the Far East generally. This situation remains stable so long as none of the creditors cry 'Wolf' and say 'Hi, we are fed up with putting our savings into falling dollars, working hard so that Americans can lie on the beach all day.' It is clearly not sustainable for ever.

Greenspan's softly, softly approach to readjusting the imbalances is likely to keep world growth on a considerably more even keel than a sharp contraction of the US economy. The risk seems well worth the potential benefit, compared to the disruption of a harsher conventional alternative. The main thing is that if world economic growth keeps going reasonably well, then the risk of a major stock market collapse is remote. [*This was wrong – the longer you put off rectifying an unsustainable situation, the harsher the eventual pain – as it has turned out.*

*What I had not realised was that the vendor finance model of recycling the excess (mainly Chinese) savings back to the USA was not sustainable. The warning signs were there: consumers using the artificially inflated value of the housing stock as an ATM machine; the US government going on living too far beyond the nation's means; and a sense of comfort within the Fed leading to too slow a tightening of the monetary base.*]

## Market and Currency Update – 30 June
FTSE 100 – 5,051 (26 Jun)

*Hedge funds*

According to Professor Friedrich Hayek (Lady Thatcher's philosophical guiding light), the human mind cannot comprehend a mechanism more complex than itself. Hence in *The Road to Serfdom* he demonstrated the inevitability of the collapse of the Command Economies because the handful of super-brains would never be able to comprehend a mechanism that involved the daily decisions of millions of brains.

Likewise, the hedge fund managers, who see themselves as super-brains (and few are backwards in coming forwards on this score), believe they can make money by 'outwitting the market'. If you believe that then you should buy them.

On this last point it is to be remarked that almost all recent hedge funds are marketed on an extremely short track record. As the record lengthens so the magic has a nasty way of vanishing.

Last month in London, GLC, Europe's largest hedge fund manager, admitted that 'flaws' in its trading models were partly to blame for the 14.5% drop in a month in the value of its credit fund. Meanwhile Bailey Coates, the fashionable West End hedge fund manager, announced the closing of its $1.3 Flagship Cromwell fund after poor returns. Man Capital in California, a convertible bond fund, is closing 'due to lack of opportunities', and Aman Capital of Singapore, manager of a macro fund, said it had ceased trading after sustaining losses in derivatives. Bailey Coates actually blamed its woes on 'other hedge funds shorting the stocks it held'!

All this brings one back to where to invest. Usually a valuable contrary indicator is what the government does (certainly the UK government). It announced last week that the new National Pension Fund compensation scheme, which it is setting up with an annual levy on all 'final salary' pension schemes in the UK (i.e. the industry must pay for its own compensation fund – not unreasonably) 'will not invest in equities at all', but hold all its assets in cash and government bonds – arguably the two fastest depreciating assets of the last 50 years.

That must mean equities are likely to be the best bet against wealth attrition in the years to come.

## Market and Currency Update – 1 December
FTSE 100 – 5,540 (close 28 Nov)

Perhaps we have seen an important pointer to the outlook for stock markets in 2006 this month with the collapse of house-building shares in the US market. It appears that the US residential property bubble may well and truly have burst, and US citizens will no longer be using their 'house equity' as an ATM machine.

Because in recent years as much as 2% of consumer spending in the US has arisen from household equity withdrawal, the cessation of this artificial stimulus may lead to a mild US recession.

As interest rate changes take at least six months to work their way through the system, the rise from under 2% to over 4% in the Fed rate in 2005 may actually only impact in 2006. This could have implications for the international level of the US dollar.

According to Barbara Tuchman in *The March of Folly* there are frequent examples in history of governments doing the opposite of what is in the best interest of their citizens. One of her main examples is the persistence of several US administrations in continuing the Vietnam War for 20 years, costing the US $150 billion, 45,000 lives and 200,000 wounded. She also cites the British wilfully losing America in 1786, by insisting on the right to levy piffling taxes on its colonies' domestic trade; the sum raised would not represent even one hundredth of the loss of business to the mother country if the colonies declared independence.

In the absence of some such folly, the US dollar should not collapse, and a recession which may weaken the dollar short term should bolster it medium term by purging some of the current spending excesses out of the domestic US market.

As to the current level of markets – both equity and bonds – it is worth looking at the current statistics.

*Bonds*

The current 'real' yield on UK index-linked bonds is 1.1% and under 1% for the recent UK 50-year issue. The return of US Treasury bonds over the last 25 years (from 1980) was 10.43%. For that return to continue for the next ten years, the yield at the end of that period would have to have fallen to 1.1%, and by 2018, to zero.

The same principle applies to corporate bonds. To repeat the past 25 years' 11.72% annual return, current yields would need to fall to 1.6% by 2015 and zero by 2025.

Anybody who believes this will happen, let them buy bonds.

[*Future potential returns for both stocks and bonds were now looking miserly; the first concrete signs of problems ahead had arrived with the US housing market starting to collapse, and Roger Bootle (City economist and Telegraph columnist) rightly warning of recession ahead.*

*At the end of 2005 the first cracks caused by the imbalances within the world economy were beginning to show. The US housing bubble had started to burst. The vendor finance model by which China effectively lent the USA more and more money to enable it to go on buying Chinese exports was stretching credibility in the dollar more and more. The consequent rapid Chinese growth (too rapid) was fuelling a commodity boom. So the imbalances were creating more imbalances, thus destabilising the system further. The Fed was tightening slowly, and this should have started to dampen everything down. In 2006 it didn't, so the stock market went on up, the FTSE 100 gaining 10.7%. A much more spectacular performance was put in by the commodity related areas – commodity stocks rose 30% and emerging markets, as a play on commodities, had a spectacular year too, up more than 30% in some cases.*

*Nobody really stopped to ask why the Fed tightening was not cooling things off or noticed that a huge shadow banking system was adding credit as fast as the Fed was removing it.*

*Markets are fed by money and there was plenty around, so on up they went, and of course profits, with the exception of one or two areas like US house-builders, were rising too. There was no sign of a property let up in the UK.]*

# 12

## *2006*

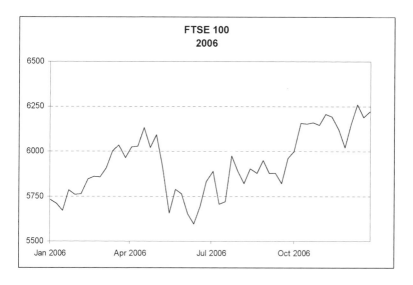

**FTSE 100**
**2006**

Figure 38

**Market and Currency Update – 1 January**
FTSE 100 – 5,618 (the FTSE has risen 16.7% in the last year)

This is the traditional time of year when everybody makes their predictions for the coming 12 months. Over the years,

143

having watched the outcome of these annual exercises in fortune telling, I can conclude that as a guide to future investment they have proved of singularly little value.

Nobody out there that I have ever come across has been right long enough to be worth following. The truth is that 'macro' will always remain incredibly difficult to foresee. It will always be skewed away from rational predictions by unforeseen or unforeseeable events

So what is 2006 likely to hold in store? The reality check is as follows:

*London*

The current bull market in London is now 32 months old and the FTSE 100 has risen from a pre-Iraq War low of 3,250 to 5,600 ( + 72%). In the last 40 years bull markets have averaged 25 months in duration, and only two have exceeded 31 months.

The forward PE looks to be around 15, which is historically neither cheap nor unreasonably expensive.

*World markets*

In general most of the emerging markets – Russia, Turkey, Brazil, India, Korea, Egypt, Eastern Europe – have had a spectacular year and are all standing towards the top end of historical valuations.

Wall Street has gone nowhere this year, but the feature has been the 'unexpected' rise in the dollar. It is now more reasonably valued as earnings have risen. The Federal Reserve continues to rein in the excess liquidity it unleashed from 2003 onwards to avoid world deflation. Much of the rise of emerging markets and capital assets everywhere, including a near worldwide property boom, is related to that release of liquidity.

This is now being reduced!

The further extent of this reduction may be a key feature to markets and asset values generally in 2006.

From the equity and property value levels at which we are starting 2006, it looks to be a tougher year in prospect for finding assets that will rise further, or as much as they have done this year.

## Market and Currency Update – 1 March
FTSE 100 – 5,842

Is it time just to play 'bridge'?

Warren Buffet famously remarked in 2000 that he had spent most of the year playing 'bridge', because looking for good value investments was a waste of time as the markets were too dear.

There is a growing feeling among those who have been around a long time in the investment world, and have to survive by being more right than wrong, rather than tracking a benchmark, that in some stock market areas investors' risk tolerance has got dangerously high.

In particular, markets have become rather polarised, as they did in the dot-com boom. Everybody wants to be in the in-fashion sectors: emerging markets, mining, energy and Japan. (Re: the latter, this position has recently changed as the Japanese market has been falling due to 'fears of overseas investors pulling out their money'.)

This brings me on to some very revealing research done by Lehavy and Sloan, published in 2005 and entitled *Investor Recognition and Stock Returns*. They found that (for the US market, which they studied) the stocks that fund managers were buying were outperformed by the stocks that fund managers were selling. This will be truer of the UK market where more institutional fund managers appear to enjoy a direct hereditary link back to the 'sheep species'.

To return to current high-ish markets, equity investors at all times have to live with the 'Armageddon' scenario because it happened once, in 1929, when they lost about 75% of their money, and the world economy collapsed too.

But, with the exception of 1929, equities seem to have inhabited a macro climate since equity markets began seriously about 150 years ago, in which every 30 to 35 years they have a crash, regardless of the economic background. This seems to be endemic to the asset class.

Currently there is fairly solid support for equity markets in general, especially where, as in many traditional industries, companies are currently trading on reasonable price earnings – well below 15. But hot spots are developing.

When the 'correction' to this big rally finally materialises, the doomsters will be out in force predicting meltdown, but one's faith in equities to deliver better longer-term returns should not be shaken. That said, it's best not to be left holding too many overvalued shares when the correction does come.

*[My thinking at the time was that 2001/2003 was the big 30-year stock market 'bust' event after 20 years of boom. That particular period of euphoria had ended in 'BUST', and therefore we were now in the early stages of the next 30-year bull market.*

*It did look as if the first stage recovery from the 2003 'bust' had been too good and too large to be sustainable, which was why I was preaching caution and taking some money off the table. But I had not realised that the asset market generally, and particularly property, had been grossly over-stimulated by excessive growth of the money supply from far too loose monetary policy both in the US and Japan.*

146

*As a result assets were becoming valued not on their worth but on the amount of money chasing them. I was still not aware that the banks, by concealed additional leverage (as happened before 1929), were adding a dangerous amount of extra fuel. This was nullifying what tightening the Fed was carrying out.*

*So when markets had a setback in 2008 I took it to be the retracement that was overdue and what you get in a bull market. So I thought that anywhere below 5,000 was becoming a buying opportunity.*

*When Lehman Brothers collapsed along with the whole rotten core of the financial sector, and the true extent of the financial excesses was suddenly revealed, one's eyes were rudely opened to the seriousness of the situation. Suddenly it became apparent that the retracement would be no 20% affair and that one would have to think again, and quickly.*]

## Market and Currency Update – 1 August
FTSE 100 – 5,950

Brian Fabbri, Chief US Economist of BNP Paribas, a leading French bank, has predicted that the US economy will slow 'precipitously' in the second half of 2006. Of course, we know how much the French love the Americans, so they might not actually be shedding that many tears over the possibility. Nevertheless it is a prediction that has to be examined seriously as there are certainly implications for profits going forward and investment valuations.

The US consumer has put up a heroic spending performance for rather a long time, and the Fed has progressively been blocking off the financial drinking wells from which he (or she) has been replenishing his (or her) spending power. Sixteen increases in Fed rates from 1% to 5.25% have tightened the screw on borrowers, and made new borrowing much more costly.

# 13

## *2007*

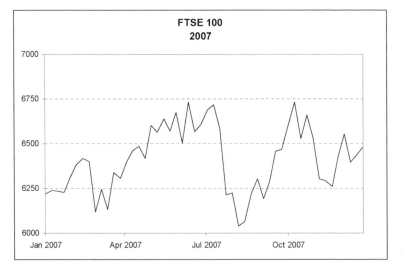

**Figure 39**

*[The year 2006 turned out to be another good one for equities generally and this had much to do with monetary policy that was much looser than we realised (partly due to mystery credit creation within the banking industry). The money was flowing back into the markets through banks lending lavishly to private equity management buyouts, take-overs and other corporate*

148

dealings where banks could earn an immediate upfront fee
(thus more bonuses).

So 2006, which should have been the year when markets
retraced and anticipated a recession as the Fed tightened,
wasn't. The following year, however, turned out to be the one in
which the excesses, now enhanced by another year of credit
creation, began to fracture, and of course from a somewhat
higher and more dangerous level. The chart above (Fig. 39),
with a double turn, was by the end of the year to indicate that
the bull run was weakening and the next leg would be
downward.]

**Market and Currency Update – 1 March**
FTSE 100 – 6,445 (26 Feb)

Headline from German newspaper, *Die Welt* (translated):
'*Delegates to global warming conference cut off by snowdrifts.*'

American journalist, essayist and satirist, H.L. Mencken
once said: 'The whole aim of practical politics is to keep the
populace alarmed (and hence clamorous to be led to safety)
by menacing it with an endless series of hobgoblins, all of
them imaginary.'

Politicians of all parties are doing this in spades with global
warming. They are falling over each other in painting apoc-
alyptic pictures of us roasting to death imminently as tem-
peratures soar; that is if we have not already been drowned
by rising sea levels. [*Scroll on to 4 December, 2010 – The Daily
Telegraph today printed an article headed 'Risk of sea level rise
now downgraded by official bodies.'*]

The lead politico for the global warming lobby is none
other of course than that great self-appointed scientific suc-
cessor to Isaac Newton, Al Gore himself. He has won an
Oscar for his film *An Inconvenient Truth*. The only thing that
is 'inconvenient' about the film is that it is most certainly not
'The Truth'.

But even to utter such thoughts invites instant damnation. *Financial Times* columnist Samuel Brittan writes:

> All I would say about the main argument is that the attempt to ignore or silence dissenters is more reminiscent of the Mediaeval Church's crusade against the Albigensian heresy than of the free enquiry of The Enlightenment.

It is now heresy to query the 'self-evident' certainty: namely, that human generated greenhouse gases are the prime cause of global warming. This, in spite of the fact that in 1998 more than 18,000 US scientists including 62 Nobel Prize winners signed a petition which argued that global warming was rooted 'in unfounded panic mongering based on flawed ideas'.

Global warming is the new moral jihad that brooks no argument against its central thesis: that man-made gases (as a by-product of capitalism) are destroying the universe. Never mind the effect of sun spots, or changes in the sun's magnetic field, or previous global warmings, such as in Roman times, when the only greenhouse gas emitted came from the camp fires of the 4th Legion, or that Greenland was a green land when found by the Vikings in 1100 – the mediaeval 'warm' period.

Ex-communists everywhere rejoice – your old philosophy of the command economy may have collapsed in the economic ruins of Eastern Europe and the USSR, but you now have a new credible Green cause to reinvigorate your favoured central controls (and accompanying explosion of bureaucrats) over the irresponsible and selfish 'free markets', which are destroying the universe.

It felt like a new ice age to the Russians last winter, which was the coldest there since 1941. The year before one third of Mongolia's livestock was wiped out by the longest cold spell they had endured in memory. But only incidents of new heat records are now permitted to be mentioned.

It must, however, be galling to the new instant experts on climate change that 2007 will not be the warmest winter on record (for the UK). That happened in 1868 when Gladstone was prime minister, and before the polluting internal combustion engine had even been invented. Of course any inconvenient data of that sort is kept well away from the public eye.

What has this got to do with the stock market? Basically it is that the Garderene instinct is easily whipped up, and is just as dangerous to sensible decisions in financial markets as it is to sensible policies from governments.

We should probably have foreseen what the gut reaction of investors would be to the double whammy equity crashes of 2001 (technology crash) and 2003 (general market fall: Dow fell from 10,000 to 7,700; FTSE 100 slumped from 6,900 to 3250). The result was that equities went from being the 20-year darling of the market to symbolising what everybody hated. One leading Swiss banker in 2003 said the correct proportion of equities in a portfolio should be: None.

So some existing money and much new investment money went into other investments. This basically boiled down to property (worldwide), private equity, and for some, hedge funds (the few that were around in 2003 had done well because they were mainly 'short' plays and finally had three good years after twenty ordinary ones when equities had gone on defying gravity). But critically they did well in the year everybody else came a cropper, and so they suddenly seemed to be the answer to everybody's dreams. Hedge funds, it was widely claimed, could and would make money whether markets went up or down. That sounded too good to miss for investors recently battered by the 2003 sell-off. Since then, the annual performance of the Funds of Hedge Funds has actually been lamentable (but their kick-back fees to intermediaries have been far from such; they have been the highest in the industry).

| Year | Fund of hedge funds | FTSE 100 | FTSE 250 |
|------|--------------------|----------|----------|
| 2004 | 6.9% | 7.0% | 18.9% |
| 2005 | 7.6% | 19.9% | 28.0% |
| 2006 | 4.9% | 13.1% | 21.0% |

**Figure 40**

Property, however, is the really big one, and since 2003 it has been attracting steadily more investment money year after year, particularly from the big institutions. TR Property Fund in its annual report of 2006 wrote:

> The fierce pace of investor demand for commercial property has shown no let up despite the recent rise in borrowing costs. From this I have to conclude that either the market is temporarily insane, or that there are other powerful factors at work leading buyers to continue to pour capital into real estate despite the absence of yield advantage over bonds.

It all has the makings of that fateful phrase: 'It's different this time.'

Paradoxically, equities are not only safest when they are hated (because by definition they are cheap) but very often do best of all asset classes. It was in 1982 that *Time Magazine* published its famous article: 'The Death of the Equity Cult.' It went on to state that alternative investments were the place to be; among others, gold, then approaching $800 an ounce. (It still has not reached that figure in nominal terms let alone real terms 25 years on.)

That article marked the start of the biggest equity boom in the American stock market's 200-year history – the Dow-Jones rising from 1,000 to over 10,000 20 years later. It was the worst advice that possibly could have been given, yet at the time it carried the full blessing of many leading financial commentators, professional advisors and virtually all bank advisors.

## Market and Currency Update – 1 April
FTSE 100 – 6,292 (28 March)

A spell in the Far East is revealing in emphasising the change in axis of economic power and growth away from Europe and into the dollar block – now the epicentre of world dynamism. That is the Big Six: USA, Japan, China, Taiwan, Singapore and Hong Kong; and what might be described as the minor planets in this economic solar system – Malaysia, Thailand, and now Vietnam starting up. The Philippines and Indonesia are still grappling with political systems that gravely restrict their ability to mirror the bustling free market economies of the leaders.

India is a separate, smaller planetary system with only $800 billion of GDP (smaller than the combined GDP of Belgium and the Netherlands – £1 trillion); but with 7% annual projected growth it will double to $1.6 trillion in ten years and probably about $3 trillion in 20.)

The combined GDPs of the Big Six now dwarfs that of Europe anyway: USA at $12.4 trillion, China at $2.2 trillion, Japan at $4.5 trillion, Taiwan at $346 billion, Hong Kong at $177 billion and Singapore at $116 billion. Total: $19,895 trillion! By comparison, the combined GDPs of the European Union nations 'only' totals $13,502 trillion.

(Figures for year ended 31 December, 2005.)

*[China in 2010 has a GDP larger than Japan at over $4 trillion.]*

The Big Six are drawing further and further away as the years move on. The ten-year plan emanating from the European

Commission to make Europe the technological leader of the world is just so much hot air expelled by Europe's proliferation of civil servants – what the French cynically call 'fonctionaires' (people who function at the expense of everyone else).

The transfer of the world's economic epicentre away from Europe is also obvious from the different mental attitudes in the two zones. Asians on the whole see the prospects for future economic growth as a glass half full (and filling); Europeans see it all too often as half empty.

This is very evident in the financial commentators sector where we never cease to be regaled by stock market doom-mongers – Andrew Smithers – the well-respected head of his eponymous think tank that has been telling us for four years that the US economy is fundamentally unsound, and that corporate profits cannot possibly continue to take such a high proportion of GDP and must fall. *Ergo*, the US stock market is grossly overvalued and riding for an immense fall. But he was saying this four years ago when the Dow was below 8,000 and the NASDAQ 40% lower than today.

[*Andrew Smithers' analysis was all too accurate but his warnings fell on deaf ears, mine included, because the markets kept on going up and seemed to be proving him wrong – and it is extraordinarily difficult to resist the sucking effect of rising markets, not least from clients who don't want to be left out when all their friends are boasting about how much money they are making in the stock market or wherever it is that's booming – like property. We were already getting to the time when the main topic of conversation at London dinner parties was how much house prices had risen since the last dinner party.*]

There are plenty of pockets of dynamism in Europe within an overall picture of regulatory sclerosis. Of course there is also

154

the issue of age. Europe has a much larger proportion of old people than Asia. But there are too many young in Europe who expect the state to hand out everything to them, from free university education to guaranteed jobs. It is hardly an attitude conducive to dynamic economic performance. No young person in the Far East (or at least very few) for a moment imagines the world owes him or her a living.


**Market and Currency Update – 1 June**
FTSE 100 – 6,606 (29 May)

No fewer than 30 FTSE 100 companies are subject to some kind of take-over rumour, or restructuring, or actual take-over (Hanson, Reuters), or private equity buyout (Allied Boots). In terms of market cap we are talking around £300 billion in play! – a figure that even the bloated private equity industry would be pushed to find, albeit 'Goldmine' Sachs have raised a whopping $20 billion and Blackstone $18 billion in the last month.

Here is a list of a few of them: Rio Tinto, Compass, Wolseley, Standard Life, Prudential, Scottish & Newcastle Pub Company, Morrisons, Drax Group.

The whole private equity industry is alleged to have raised £150 billion last year, but that covers the world's stock markets, and the UK market represents a mere 10% of world market capitalisation.

Meanwhile the IMF warns that a private equity collapse is on the cards, and has predicted that many of the current deals being mulled over could prove a disappointment.

[*How right the IMF was – they were being badly executed at too high prices with too much gearing because the incentives had gone all wrong. Bankers were getting their remuneration from up-front arrangement fees, with no interest in the success or failure of the outcome. Markets were suckers for absorbing the high coupon debt issued; interest rates were not high enough so that made the strong yields attractive. The risks were overlooked, and the banks could offload the loans given almost overnight (at least until the music stopped). So risk officers could be lulled into believing the bridging loan was riskless. But the music did stop – extremely abruptly. These loans overnight became as immovable as set concrete.*

*Investors, having given the private equity groups too much money, had no control over how it was spent.*]

But until one bridging loan goes badly wrong the banks will probably go on with their relatively lax financing of them; then, sheep that they are, they will all tighten up simultaneously, removing a not inconsiderable prop from stock markets.

But the point made above is that the speculation has driven too many stock prices to levels only sustainable in the event of a bid. As they cannot possibly all be bid for, a lot of these stocks are likely to fall back to a fair value level. This could be 10–15% below current levels. Meanwhile, technically, the market is comfortably (or rather uncomfortably) above both its 50-day and 200-day moving average – i.e. it is over-bought. With the summer months coming up, always a more dodgy period for markets to navigate, the likelihood of some kind of correction looks quite high.

## Market and Currency Update – 1 August

| | | |
|---|---|---|
| FTSE 100 | 1 January 2007 | 6,220 |
| FTSE 100 | 1 July 2007 | 6,640  +6.7% |
| FTSE 100 | 29 July 2007 | 6,212 -6.5% |

**Figure 41**

The above demonstrates very clearly what has happened in the last ten days: the year's gains have vanished in the correction, long predicted and finally here after enough investors decided that it would *not* happen and threw in their last chips.

Big property investors like Standard Life and Scottish Widows had to close their property funds because they were swamped with more money than they could find sensible investments in which to put it. So these unwanted surpluses swilled off into the Alternative Investment Market (AIM), where less scrupulous operators happily dreamed up vehicles, many somewhat dubious, with which to mop them up. 'Bulgarian', 'Ottoman', 'Romanian' – you name it – property funds sprouted like mushrooms in the night; and like mushrooms, they might just have a rather short life. Altogether £7 billion was raised on AIM for these wonderful ventures, the shares from most of which are now lingering at a discount to the issue price.

Then the worldwide housing boom led to houses being used as cash machines, fuelling unsustainable consumer demand and inflation.

The worst aspect of the private equity bubble was that it shifted where the profit of the big private equity houses was coming from. Previously it came from their own capital invested alongside the institutions plus their arrangement fees. Now the lion's share was coming from the arrangement fees as the volume of money showered on them was so great that the deals ran into hundreds of millions and their own capital stayed in the bank, being too small to play a meaningful part. Hence the willingness of these organisations to take businesses – and very large ones like Boots – private at hefty prices just to place the piles of cash and get their fees. Nobody worries too much about how they spend other people's money.

Meanwhile the banks were getting succulent fees for arranging the debt finance. They knew that the low quality, poorly secured loans they were financing and, hopefully passing on, might eventually go sour, but not for a year or three, whereas the fat fees went to the bottom line immediately, ballooning their bonuses. This toxic loan build-up was drawn attention to by British investment fund manager, Anthony Bolton, a few months ago.

When rising US interest rates finally punctured the dodgy sub prime market, the big corporate bankers to the private equity industry bonanza suddenly found themselves without a chair to sit on, and the music had ceased altogether.

Getting rid of $20 billion or so of these weak loans is now going to cost these banks all the juicy fees they have earned in the last 12 months, and the bonuses already taken won't be paid back. There is something really toxic about the remuneration system here.

The bubble is over in the USA – no more false boosting of consumer spending via remortgaging the rising house values (now falling). Spain was hit next, and the UK stock market has taken the view since last January that the game is soon to be up in Britain also.

**Market and Currency Update – 1 September**
FTSE 100 – 6,310

The following was written in the *Sunday Telegraph* on 26 August: 'Pension fund trustees are planning legal action against several London hedge funds in a desperate bid to salvage investments threatened by the recent credit crunch.'

What on earth were pension funds doing putting their money into hedge funds in the first place? Well, Arnold Van Den Berg, of Century Capital, a legendary US investor in the Warren Buffet mould, who have steered their clients' money successfully through all the big market set-backs of the last 30 years) wrote in his annual letter of April 2004: 'Pension funds are the last to get sucked in but when they do, boy does the money gush in.'

He goes on:

> Let me tell you something about pension funds –
> because they are a wonderful indicator. Pension funds
> are designed to protect you so they have the most con-
> servative laws.

So whenever a new fad starts the pension fund industry never gets involved – because it is made up of prudent men and women. And they are not going to get sucked into a fad. So they always resist new ideas. Then a little time goes by and they get pressure from the people they manage the plan for. They say, 'Look, stocks haven't done well, bonds haven't done well but gold and diamonds are up' – so they have meetings. However, nothing happens, they vote it down.

But eventually pressure becomes irresistible. More people come in, brokerage houses' reports start to pour out, and universities start looking at new ideas and see how well they have gone, and how poorly the old ones have done.

And now it just keeps going and going. Once it becomes a mania all bets are off. There is no way that the trustees of the pension fund can resist. And that is why these pension funds get in at the tail end of 'whatever it is'; because they are the last ones to be converted.

Van Den Berg continues: 'The latest big idea? Hedge funds.' (This was written in 2004.) 'It's an idea that's been around for 50 years but it's only gotten a new lease of life in the last 5. Basically what hedge funds can do is use any conceivable speculative idea known to man. And they can make huge amounts of money. And they can lose huge amounts of money.

The great thing about hedge funds is that they are not regulated, and do not have to report to governments. So they can do what they want.

So you can just imagine the sort of things in which they are invested. And because of their track record (they did well in 2000 to 2003 when stock markets collapsed) these pension funds are moving into them in a big way.'

Well it has taken just three short years from what Van Den Berg called 'the tail end of whatever it is' – during which, incidentally, Funds of Hedge Fund returns have been abysmal, and have been outpaced by the indices of almost all major stock markets – for the chickens to come home to roost in the hedge fund sector.

There is an (insufficiently) well-known investment book written by Nicholas Taleb, a professor of mathematics at Yale, entitled *Foiled by Randomness.*

As Taleb argues in his book, computers can only programme what has happened in the past. But by definition what always moves financial markets unexpectedly is what has NOT happened before. Trying to permanently outwit markets is like trying to beat the roulette wheel. Many have claimed to have created a foolproof mathematical system to do just that, and then ended as 'waiters' in the casino where they tried it.

Unfortunately, in the case of hedge funds, it is more likely that the investors end up as 'waiters' because the managers have stacked up so much in fees that they can probably walk away unscathed.

In a lifetime of involvement with financial markets I cannot remember a bigger 'con' that has been visited on the investment community than the claim: 'We can make you money whether markets go up or down.' Luckily this myth is now imploding, and hopefully before too many small retail investors get sucked in. A dedicated website now exists to enable anyone to track the fall-out: www.hedgefund implode.com.

**Figure 42**

## Market and Currency Update – 1 October
FTSE 100 – 6,467

Annual inflation of 4% can wipe a third off the buying power of £1,000 within ten years.

We all know that real inflation, as opposed to the doctored figures of our governments, has been running at about this level for several years; for instance council tax in the UK has doubled in the last ten years (i.e. annual compound inflation rate of 7%).

Some of my clients have always taken the view that basically all governments are spendthrifts and the only financial certainty in life is the steady fall in the purchasing power of virtually all currencies. So to preserve capital let alone increase it, the only place to be is in real assets: equities and real estate.

Accepting the ups and downs, panics and euphoria of equities and real estate is far and away better than having one's wealth relentlessly eroded by holding paper money – whomever it belongs to.

The only losers from this long-term policy are those that adopt it and then get panicked out in the periodic switch-backs that equity markets go through. Avoiding this latter pitfall is one of the key factors in good long-term equity performance.

The current recovery in markets emphasises yet again just how the axis of economic power has shifted away from Europe to the Pacific. This is where markets are strongest, and they have led the recovery worldwide. The Pacific area, including the USA, is now economically almost twice as large as Europe. Indeed the Pacific territory on its own is now probably large enough for the first time to absorb an American slowdown, without being pitched into recession itself. Throw in the buoyancy of the non-Asian emerging markets – Latin America, Russia and its resource-rich neighbour states plus the Gulf states – and much of the world is firing very strongly.

So are we out of the woods or is this a sucker's rally?

*[It looked as if the corrosion in financial markets was being contained but what very few of us realised, and I did not, was that so much debt had been built up inside the banking system, and that the banking reserves were not remotely large enough to absorb the derivative-inflated bad debts developing in the property fall-out in the US (and Spain) on top of their hope-lessly swollen balance sheets.*

*Whereas, for example, Chinese and Indian banks were only*

*lending 70% of their deposits, RBS, HBOS, Citibank and others, including, notoriously, Northern Rock, were lending 140% of their deposits, and Lehman, about 1,000%!*

*We did not realise just how close we were to the edge of the precipice; little comfort that the financial regulators had not seen it either.*]

## Market and Currency Update – 1 December
FTSE 100 – 6,350

'My right is falling back, my left is caving in. My centre is under pressure – situation excellent. I attack.'

These were the words of one of the better commanders in the First World War (Marshal Foch) in the middle of a battle, which he subsequently won.

Investors might have been feeling the same recently. Banks and associated financial institutions have been crumbling worldwide. Property and house-building shares have been collapsing on both sides of the Atlantic, and the 'Centre' – i.e. the American economy – is on the 'wobble'.

Over the long term, stock markets tend to have followed a fairly consistent 20–30-year cycle of behaviour (and the same applies to individual stocks or stock market sectors), which roughly equates to four phases; their lengths vary but the nature of the phases seems to have been one of the rare predictabilities of equity markets. These are: revulsion, caution, enthusiasm, euphoria, (bust).

Bust is not a phase because it happens suddenly and unexpectedly and so quickly. It can be as little as one day in the case of an individual stock, or six months in the case of an entire market; or, as in 1987, five and a half hours (that was actually the length of the bear market on Wall Street in that year).

163

Anyway, the generality is that 90% of those in the euphoria phase who don't leave the party in time lose possibly five or ten years of hard won gains, or the late comers never see their money back.

This is exactly what has happened both in property and private equity. Everybody last year was plunging into property investment, and then came the usual sign of a 'top'; the mutual funds launched their property funds, and the bubble has already burst less than a year later. Property shares have more or less halved. M&G Investments suspended redemptions for three months and the experts are predicting that next year actual commercial property could fall by another 20%.

There is scant comfort for those, pushed into 'alternative investments in property' in the last 18 months, who are now nursing uncomfortable losses.

Returning to the stock market, unless I am wrong in calling 2001/2003 the bust at the end of a 25-year run, which started in 1975 (it went through all the phases: revulsion, caution, enthusiasm, etc.), we are still early on in the longer-term equity bull cycle. But by June 2006 the cycle seemed to have jumped from 2003 revulsion to 2006 enthusiasm rather too quickly, probably resulting from somewhat too lax Fed monetary policy. It is easy with hindsight to say this, but at the time the sharp Federal Reserve increase in money supply staved off what looked at the time (in 2003) to be the onset of a nasty deflation.

Now there are a number of problems that have got to be worked through before markets can resume a longer-term upward trend. But both the European central bank and the Fed appear utterly determined to avoid world deflation, either through forced or accidental monetary contraction. We are all Keynesians now (except Mervyn King).

[*Unfortunately the problems that had stacked up visibly were eclipsed by those that had done so invisibly. It was not long before the scales would drop from our eyes, and the benign possibility of a mild recession to rectify the excesses would become a distant mirage.*]

# 14

## *2008*

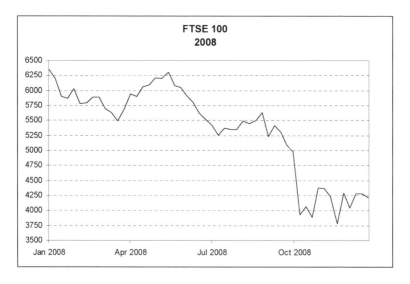

**Figure 43**

*[The year 2008 had opened at 6,456 for the FTSE 100. It was to end at 4,439, having dipped as low as 3,680 in September, when the full nakedness of the banking system was finally revealed by the Lehman Bros collapse. But as the New Year opened there was quite strong buying of both property shares and bank shares as some high profile and well-regarded fund*

166

*managers thought they had fallen enough to be at bargain levels. The general feeling was that 2008 would be a more difficult year in stock markets to make money and I had concluded my 1 January newsletter with the comment: '2008 was likely to be a more challenging year to make money but periodic swings of adverse sentiment could give some excellent buying opportunities.'*

*Practically nobody was expecting the near 50% collapse in markets, with some emerging markets (still then on the crest of a boom) falling 70% (Russia and Indonesia), and even staid Hong Kong dropping briefly from 30,000 at its peak to 11,000.]*


## Market and Currency Update – 1 February
FTSE 100 – 5,879 (31 Jan)

Volatility is the watchword of the day after the 10% fall of the FTSE 100 and other indices since 1 January. All volatility means is that the market has gone down and people don't like it.

Nobody complains when it is 'volatile' upwards. That is 'wise investment'.

Unfortunately, periodic bouts of volatility are, and have always been, the nature of the animal – prices in the short term being driven more by raw human emotion than cool, rational analysis.

Furthermore, it is not possible to predict when one of these stormy periods will happen as the timing is random, and it does not even confine itself to overvalued markets or sectors. It can even happen in already undervalued sectors.

Historically these periods of high volatility and sharp falls have proved very good buying opportunities.

It is noticeable that Warren Buffet, who had been quiescent for some considerable time, accumulating cash, has been very active in the last three months, both inside and outside the US. He clearly does not take the same Armageddon view as George Soros (Hungarian-American financier, business-man and philanthropist). Buffet does not even believe there is any point in trying to predict where the stock market is going short term or indeed the economic cycle. He buys where he sees good value.

What a refreshingly long-term approach, which should of course be taken by all pension fund managers. But it isn't, as they allow themselves to be pushed around by short-sighted regulators and actuaries, destroying long-term value as they force trustees to seek short-term but illusory safety in bonds.

One leading pension fund that refused stubbornly to veer off its long-term course in 2003, and for that matter in every other stock market squall, when nearly everybody else did, is the University Superannuation pension fund; its policy is made up of 80% equities. The fund managers claim they are investing for at least 200 years, and indeed most of the uni-versities whose staff pensions they manage, have actually been around for longer than that. They know that it is the perpetually dwindling buying power of money, currently shrinking at least 4% a year, that is the real threat to long-term returns.

Although the world economy is more integrated than ever before, and even though the burgeoning economies of the Far East know they cannot completely disassociate themselves from what goes on in the USA, the relative weights have nevertheless changed fairly radically in the last decade. That is the big difference.

This probably means that if we do have a recession in the West, for the first time the emerging and Asian economies are large enough to help pull us out. In the past the West has just had to work through it, meaning it takes longer, as in 1990–1993.

Of all the economies, the UK looks to be one of the worst placed as we go into this downturn. Whilst the corporate

168

sector has a very healthy balance sheet (though the position of the banks is not yet clear) that of the government is positively sick; also consumer debt is slightly higher than in the US and considerably higher than Continental Europe, excepting possibly Spain.

The Continental European economy looks in significantly more robust shape, with Germany having virtually eliminated its budget deficit, and France at least having frozen hers. Meanwhile the UK alone has, under Brown, let it balloon.

France also, being the largest agricultural economy in Europe (about 8% of the French economy), stands to benefit substantially from the surging agricultural prices. In the UK this urban government has gone out of its way to grind the remnants of the British farming industry into the mire, where it currently represents less than 2% of GDP.

There is no chance of tax cuts, nor any other fiscal stimulus to help the UK economy. Whatever happens internationally, a sharp downturn here almost looks a certainty.

The stock market may in fact have already got the measure of this, bearing in mind that UK retail stocks are selling at the lowest multiple of sales ever.

The governor of the Bank of England may, however, be right to maintain that the over-borrowing binge is utterly unsustainable; and uncomfortable though it may be, the sooner a sustainable level of savings is achieved, the quicker long-term recovery will be possible.

A permanently higher savings ratio is necessary in the US too, and there is some scepticism that aggressive reduction of interest rates may only defer the inevitable adjustment. But a deflationary spiral starts to destroy wealth on an epic scale, and the Fed has to make a balanced judgement.

Whilst the short-term outlook is very confused, in general things neither turn out as bad as the pessimists insist, nor as well as the optimists hope.

Barring some seismic event, the world economy has a way

of chugging along through good and difficult times at 2–4% growth, and with the new dynamism of the emerging economies perhaps the whole is more balanced than the current alarmism would suggest. [*Unfortunately a seismic event which few of us foresaw was just round the corner.*]

Neil Collins, the very astute former financial editor of *The Telegraph* – now writing with Anthony Hilton for the *Evening Standard* – wrote on 24 January: 'Are we in the stock market spin cycle, or merely approaching the final rinse?'

He goes on:

As the gains of the last few years are washed away, and George Soros writes about the apocalypse now, it is easy to see why investors are rushing into what seems to be the safety of government bonds. Alas, as usual with investment rushes, they are almost certainly rushing the wrong way.

He concludes:

Nobody can pick the turn of the market except by luck, but there is plenty of nice clean value out there among those stocks that have already finished their spin cycle.

**Market and Currency Update – 1 July**
FTSE 100 – 5,500

At 1 July, 2007 the index was standing at 6,549. It is now a thousand points lower. Kick out the oil and mining shares and it would be over 2,000 points lower. For the UK domestic shares market – banks, property, house builders, retail – there has been about a 60% drop. That is already a massive bear market by any measure.

This reflects people's fears generally that UK PLC goes

into this current economic downturn in worse shape than almost any other major economy.

There is no need to dwell on the relative weakness of the UK, which can be summed up in one word: Brown (but the fiscal damage was done when he was at the Treasury). Italy is at least one better – with nobody in charge.

France and Germany, not to mention Switzerland and the Scandinavian countries, all look in much more solid shape. But everybody is suffering with oil having doubled again. Few foresaw this last October, or believed it would be anything more than a spike. Now everyone is assuming we are stuck with high oil indefinitely, and that is what has spooked the market since March. If that turns out to be wrong then markets could turn round equally sharply. But whether it is spooked enough or too much at today's level, it is impossible to more than make a blind guess at.

Sir John Ritblat (who steered The British Land Company from assets of £6 million in 1971, when he started, to £10 billion by 2006 when he retired) has been the successful survivor of three such property boom/busts in his life. He has sensible words on how to survive: 'Markets,' he says, 'are like rabbits in headlights. They get fixated. The trick is just to sit it out. You cannot beat markets when markets are going down – dynamite won't shift them. Just go away and ski or play golf.' (He does both very well and is one of the rare sponsors of young British skiers.)

But just as he rightly says dynamite won't shift falling markets, equally quixotically, when they turn, they behave like quicksilver. One moment it's here; the next it is gone. Most of those who sold out in 2003 did not start to return until 2006, by which time the market had in many places more than doubled. Indeed they just got back in time for the next downturn.

Making money is always difficult, and as a vehicle for doing so the stock market is as difficult as any; what is

171

deceiving is that at times it gives the false impression of being dead easy. But trying to outwit markets is a mug's game as the ever rising roll-call of hedge funds rolling over testifies.

Warren Buffet claims he ignores market movements completely and concentrates on finding the right businesses to invest in. By 'right' he means a combination of a good business purchased at the right price. There are certainly plenty of those around at the moment in these current depressed markets.

## Market and Currency Update – 1 September
FTSE 100 – 5,531

Humpty Dumpty is going to take some time to be put back together again. Too much capital destruction has happened as a result of the incredible credit excesses of the capital markets. A significant slug of tomorrow's consumption was already consumed yesterday. On top of this, continuing extraordinary financial irresponsibility (mainly from investment banking) has nearly shot the world economy in the foot again this spring, as these organisations recklessly incite the public to 'invest in commodities'.

Fortunately, whilst the Federal Reserve had its hands tied – being literally forced to loosen credit to avoid a financial collapse – the European Central Bank made what in retrospect may prove to have been a brilliant move. It raised interest rates even as recession in Europe loomed. This cut European demand quickly and enough to stem Chinese growth, Europe now being China's largest export market; subsequently freight rates halved, real demand for most major commodities fell off quickly, and the speculators' dangerous bubble has been quickly burst.

Now in the very short term a lot of commodity prices may undershoot their underlying market equilibrium price as the commodity funds are forced sellers.

172

Alan Greenspan did not believe in bursting bubbles but dealing with the aftermath once market forces had finally made it happen. But this thinking may well have to change in future, because since the abolition of the Glass-Steagall Act (by Clinton) the floodgates were reopened, allowing the capacity of the financial system to gamble on a colossal scale.

This is what happened in 1929 when, as Maynard Keynes observed, 'enterprise had become the bubbles on a whirlpool of speculation, instead of speculation being the bubbles on a sea of enterprise'.

The monetary guru, Professor Charles Goodhart – former MPC member (Monetary Policy Committee) – has contributed a level-headed assessment of the current outlook rather than the more alarmist approach favoured by the press. Bad news sells much better than good news, so ever since markets started falling we have been bombarded almost daily with the most wild and unbalanced predictions of eminent Armageddon specialists. They, like sewage, always rise to the surface when a pond gets stirred.

Professor Goodhart is referring principally to the UK economy and indicating the likely extent of the coming recession and its comparability with that of 1991. Without intending to distort genuine wisdom by naive compression, his main point is that the early fall in sterling will cushion somewhat the necessary readjustment, unlike in the early 1990s when we were stuck shadowing the ERM (European Exchange Rate Mechanism). He thinks that by the turn of the year inflation figures may start to look very much better, enabling interest rate cuts, possibly in the New Year. He has warned that 'the worst depressions result from financial collapses' and that financial instability remains a downside danger to the world economy. [*This was a perceptive warning as the financial excesses turned out to be so great that they were not containable and were shortly to burst wide open with the Lehman collapse, and collapse in all but name of the western banking system.*]

Markets generally are also beginning to show signs of ignoring bad news, but after so much turmoil and so much volatility quite a prolonged period of convalescence may well be required before a new bull market re-emerges.

## Market and Currency Update – 1 October
FTSE 100 – 4,895

In the more than 20 years I have been writing this monthly newsletter, this is without doubt the most difficult one to do.

Since last month a seismic change has happened in the financial world, taking it well outside the parameters experienced in our lifetimes.

All the careful controls put in place for the banking system after the financial collapse of 1929, in order to avoid such an event ever happening again, have failed, and during August the financial 'levees' gave way.

*Financial New Orleans is now under water*

The system has now flooded, and several bodies, at the very heart of the system, have already had to be stretchered away – Lehman, Merrill Lynch, Washington Mutual, Morgan Stanley, and of course AIG. That is in the US. Here in Europe we can mention HBOS, Fortis and Dexia; in this context Bradford & Bingley is too trivial to mention, just a peripheral casualty, of which there may be quite a few more. Nobody – but nobody – alive today has had to deal with this situation before, though Ben Bernanke (current Chairman of the Federal Reserve) was luckily an expert on the causes of the Great Crash.

Without the US Federal Reserve's prompt action from the very beginning we would by now be in a considerably worse position than we actually are, uncomfortable as it is. The $800 billion package is clearly the right response to the enhanced deterioration, and will probably go through. The revulsion of the US public to bailing out the greedy and so far unrepentant sinners who have brought this about is understandable, but there is probably no other way. It's for everybody's benefit and the retribution against the bankers can come later.

There is little doubt that, going forward, a whole new framework for banking, to include much tighter controls on leverage and possibly higher capital ratios to deposits, will be put in place, thus making for a slower expansion of credit in the future. Glass-Steagall in some new form will be implemented (it was unwisely repealed in 1999 by Clinton).

After the repeal, many retail banks took on investment banks, lured by their higher apparent profits on capital. It was not long before the investment banking tail was wagging the much bigger retail banking dog.

The retail banks just became a gigantic piece of free collateral, which the investment banking arms seized in order to massively jack up the size of their deals and dealing activities, thus multiplying the fees they earned several fold. It was no longer their own capital at risk so, what the hell!

Bonuses based on fees drove traders to ever more daring excesses. Clearly too many of them, with the connivance of the bosses (also fee driven), didn't care enough about the capital risks. The result we now know. [*Remuneration incentives had gone wildly wrong because bonuses were paid on arrangement fees for loans irrespective of soundness or recklessness of the loan given. In short: the capital risks had become completely detached from the earning of the bonus.*]

In Europe, Jean-Claude Trichet, president of the European Central Bank, and its governors, have acted quickly and decisively. They effectively, from day one of this crisis, have used the central bank as an operating alternative for all the

European regulated banks to the three-month inter-bank market, which had seized up. That has kept the system going.

The Bank of England belatedly followed suit, but initially with punitive terms, which virtually assured that any bank that used its discount window would be likely to have a run on it. At last, in the latest couple of months, it has come into line but that delay probably sank Bradford & Bingley and forced HBOS into the arms of Lloyds.

The problem is that in a recession, bar the very conservative banks, most banks become technically insolvent for a while on a mark to market basis of their assets. Their deposits – the liabilities – stay the same in a recession whilst their assets – their loans and bond books, etc. – are subject to a degree of write-offs, or anyway, write-downs. This should be covered normally by their capital and reserves. On this occasion, in contrast to the recessions of 1992 or the early eighties or the seventies, many banks had in fact swollen their balance sheets way beyond the 'ten to one' capital-to-deposit ratios through off-balance sheet vehicles, derivatives and so on. Furthermore, in search for extra tax, without realising the consequences, the Inland Revenue had persuaded the Treasury after 1994 to stop the age old bank practice of making 'general reserves'.

Of course 'general reserves' reduced taxable profits, but this also strengthened banks with an extra layer of uncommitted capital. This had proved an invaluable cushion in the UK property crash of 1992.

Unfortunately, while economies were booming, all of us in the investment industry were guilty of closing our eyes to the growing signs of excess, which frankly were rather well covered up – as Enron had been.

Many of us had been cautious for some time, well aware that too many bubbles were building up – in particular in property and commodities. But to avoid these seemed sufficient. Very, very few foresaw the risk of a complete implosion of most of the world's financial system as well, or that the banks in reality had got themselves quite so overstretched.

Warren Buffet had drawn attention to the vast time bomb of derivatives that was ticking, and frankly most of us outside the banking industry did not understand quite how they worked, or that they were creating quite so much extra credit. However, we are where we are now, and that is the point from which to work.

We have to find a sensible but probably different approach going forward for investment strategy from what would be the case in a normal recession. I think it is correct to say that normality is going to take longer to re-establish itself than we could have predicted, and the risks of further financial dislocation have not gone away.

There is still a lot of unwinding to be done, particularly in the hedge fund area. It is the hedge funds primarily that have propelled speculation in commodities. Public investment in commodities had always been small – it was an inter-professional market. In 2003 it stood at about $23 billion. By the spring of this year it had ballooned to a gargantuan $670 billion. In mediaeval times hoarders of commodities in periods of scarcity had their heads cut off.

The only commodity that is a genuine investment medium is gold. Everything else is gambling froth. To try and make these into investment products and sell them to the public is nonsense, and when it gets to the sort of size it did, it is potentially very destabilising.

In the interests of humanity generally there really is a case for limiting commodity trading to professionally involved businesses only. In practice it is difficult to see how this could be implemented, as it would have to be worldwide.

All that has happened is that enough quantities of many commodities have been taken out of the supply chain, in the short term, to dislocate the normal supply/demand price mechanism. This has caused highly dislocating price spikes such as those which occurred this spring. Now the forced unwinding of this $670 billion stockpile is almost certainly pushing prices well below the real market clearing rate, and leading yet again to violently unsettling, irrational gyrations in the prices.

All these excesses are unravelling now, but it does make it quite difficult to know what the real market clearing price for such key commodities as oil, gas, wheat, corn and the big metals really is. The future rate of inflation, and the relative terms of trade between the producer and consumer nations, depend upon where these clearing prices end up.

For more than 20 years this relationship had hugely favoured the consumer nations. This now appears to have reversed. The likely sharper world downturn may subdue prices more in the short term but not back to old levels. In soft commodities a bumper European harvest has pushed feed wheat back to £90. It was £125 at harvest debut in mid August, and you could sell forward harvest wheat in July at £140. That is good news for food prices and inflation.

A sign that stock market prices in certain areas are now at levels offering serious long-term value, even allowing for further dislocating risk ahead, is that Warren Buffet has been an active buyer in the last four weeks. Firstly, he took a big stake in Goldman Sachs and yesterday bought a stake in a Chinese electric vehicle manufacturer.

Investors are in much more difficult, choppy and unsettled conditions. Retiring to the sidelines is only a temporary solution, and continuing to do so at very depressed levels could be costly.

There are some very cheap assets out there now, but the risks of further financial dislocation continue to overshadow the whole economic scene. This is making the normal assessment of risk reward ratio very much harder; it is far more difficult to separate what is genuinely cheap from what just looks cheap but isn't.

178

# 15

## 2009

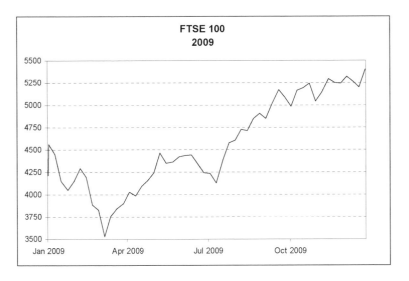

**Figure 44**

[*January 2009 began at 4,372 but the mood in the market was one of acute fear. Nobody was predicting any swift recovery in stock markets and the flight to sovereign bonds was 'the safe thing to do'. Many stocks had fallen far below bargain basement levels, indicating fears of insolvency even among companies with strong balance sheets and well-branded businesses.*

179

*The six months from the collapse of Lehman to the second (double bottom) of 2 March, 2009 (3,684) was in fact one of the greatest buying opportunities in stock market history. Such well established blue chips as Burberry could be picked up below 150p (they are now £10.) Among smaller companies there were to be within 18 months some 10 'baggers'. Cape Industries, an oil services company, could then be bought for 32p (now selling for 330p). The institutions too fearful for their liquidity ratios dared not buy equities. Cash, everybody said, was king.*

*Risk aversion was so tremendous that enormous bargains had developed in the corporate finance world – especially the bonds of financially related companies. Prudential US 6.75% perpetual bonds fell to 32 cents (now 94 cents); Old Mutual 8% perpetual bonds actually dropped to 16p at one point, yielding an astonishing 46% (now 80p); BMW had to pay 9.9% for a five-year bond issue (its yield to maturity has now dropped to 4%). Never was there a more expensive call than 'cash is king'. The opportunity of a lifetime to make huge gains very quickly was missed by nearly everybody with cash to invest.]*

### Market and Currency Update – 1 February
FTSE 100 – 4,194

Patience Wheatcroft, the distinguished former financial editor of *The Times*, described New Labour rather as New Labour Force: 'not so much an administration as a massive job creation scheme at the taxpayers expense'.

'Today,' she continues, 'will bring official confirmation that another 260,000 people joined the public sector payroll in the year to last autumn. That is more than Tesco's entire workforce and well over twice the number of people that BP, one of the world's biggest companies, employs.'

Altogether about 900,000 people have been added to the public sector workforce since Labour won power.

At some point a massive restructuring of the UK economy will have to take place – out of the public sector and back into the productive sector. It seems almost certain that we have gone over the tipping point, where those in productive work can never produce enough to pay for the ballooned public sector. Just to repeat the figures, public sector costs were £379 billion in 1998 and rose to £648 billion in 2008 (+ 70%). The economy grew 30% in the same decade.

If we cannot produce politicians with enough courage to take an axe to this abscess, it will presumably be forced on us by the IMF.

Sterling has already fallen 30% against the dollar and the euro. As the public sector continues to pile on jobs whilst the recession is shrinking the earning power of the private sector, the stock price (i.e. sterling) appears to have no direction to go in other than further downwards.

We of course live in a relative world, and if the economic figures for the US and the eurozone decline faster and further than those of the British, then relative to them the UK could remain where it is. That situation would favour gold, which some investors have already taken on board. Gold of course has already trebled from its low of $250 (when Gordon Brown sold part of the the UK's gold reserves). Inflation has certainly not yet trebled, so maybe at this price (about $900 an ounce) gold is ahead of the game. But then the question of shortage comes in.

Relative to the volume of paper currencies owned world-wide, at $900 an ounce, the world stock of gold (say 60,000 tons or 1.75 billion oz) is worth $1.57 trillion, a smidgen of the value of paper currencies.

The US annual GDP alone is over $12 trillion and the Royal Bank of Scotland's balance sheet is (or was!) £1.8 trillion. So the amount of gold is tiny relative to the pile of world paper money.

Anyway, all this gold stock is either in government vaults

or is already in private hands. The governments may sell some, but private holders seem unlikely to offload much in the current dicey economic conditions.

Annual production is running at about 2,000 tons (about 71 million oz) or, in dollar terms (at $900 an ounce), about $63 billion. That wouldn't even mop up a morning's trading in the £/$ foreign exchange market – running at $100 billion a day.

Investors have to decide for themselves how useful a slug of gold, which yields nothing, is to their financial stability in a stormy fiscal world. But clearly if any serious number of people decided that they wanted to convert their paper money into gold, the price would have to soar. On the other hand, a return sometime soon to financial stability is not good news for gold holders.

It is difficult to deduce from the current gold chart whether the present price is just a short-term correction from the recent $1,000 peak, or whether, after rising for eight years from $250, the chart is topping out.

Bearing in mind that only a year ago it seemed the world really was expanding at a rate that meant nearly all commodities were in short supply at their old prices of production, it does seem that the current drop in prices might not last long – unless we hit a depression-size recession.

Virtually all the cheap and easy deposits of most metals, and certainly oil, have now been exhausted, so replacement production, let alone additional production, is going to come in at a significantly higher price.

So cost push cost inflation could soon return, thus underpinning a higher future gold price. But other commodities, whose prices have currently collapsed, unlike that of gold, might offer better value – albeit the ordinary investor cannot readily keep a pile of wheat, or a heap of iron ore, let alone some active uranium oxide in his safe (the Health and Safety lobby would pass out!). But a flight to real assets is a genuine possibility if people actually become spooked by the volume of paper money being disgorged.

*Equities*

I would certainly say that the majority of investors still expect markets to fall further before equities start a genuine recovery. That said, the basis on which I believe that it is right to buy equities selectively from now on (now they have fallen worldwide) is as follows:

The world has gone into a major financial crisis on a scale probably greater than 1929. The great difference is that this is the second time it has happened. Thus the authorities have the benefit of knowing what not to do and what to do to prevent this financial meltdown turning a normal cyclical recession into a depression.

Too many people are making all sorts of predictions about the outcome of the financial meltdown – mainly on the pessimistic side – especially the media spearheaded by the BBC, in my opinion a stronghold of anti-capitalists. They should perhaps be reminded of what Keynes said about prediction: 'Our powers of prediction are slight; our command over results infinitesimal.'

There may be short-term pain if the current downward lurch does not steady soon, but the real professionals – Buffet, Woodford and Bolton (all with exceptional long-term records with equities) – are not sellers and have been selective buyers since the market hit 3,800 in the UK and 7,800 in the US in the late autumn.

One thing does look a high probability. When economic recovery does begin, equities will already have soared round the world. Record amounts of cash piled on the sidelines means this is almost inevitable.

History shows that people 'out of the Market' waiting for the bottom never get back in time; each rally is seen as a bear trap. Then the rally that turns into the new bull market is also avoided. By the time they realise it is a bull market the train has long gone.

## Market and Currency Update – 1 March
FTSE100 – 3,684 (2 Mar); 4,231 (1 Feb); change – 13%

There are only two things without limits according to Gurdjieff, the mystic philosopher: 'Man's stupidity and the Mercy of God'.

We have certainly suffered an unduly large portion of the former, and we are unlikely to earn the latter until human counsels show considerably greater wisdom.

As markets crumble again there is a tendency to remain pessimistic, but there are considerable grounds for hope as leaders everywhere, almost without exception, are showing considerable skill and vigour to put Humpty Dumpty back together again. This is remarkable, considering the diversity of cultures that are largely acting in unison.

Whilst there are differences in the minutiae of what is the best precise package of measures for each economy, all the major economic powers are in broad harmony on the macro thrust of what to do.

Everywhere the necessity to keep credit flowing in the real economy has been recognised. The need to prevent any further contraction in the money supply, if necessary by quantitative easing, is now virtually agreed by all. Different countries may be supporting their banking systems in different ways, but the aim is agreed and is unanimous.

The contraction in the money supply was what turned the recession of 1929/1930 into the Depression of 1933. Though today there is bound to be some political posturing over local jobs, every one of the major economies is agreed over the need to avoid a rise in general protectionism. Politicians will of course look to their own constituencies and there will inevitably be some cheating at the margin, but no general tariff obstructions as happened in the thirties.

It is tempting and easy to criticise these efforts, and make mischief by highlighting minor divisions. It would be extraordinary if there were not many, as everybody has their own ideas of how best to navigate the uncharted waters. But they are no longer that uncharted. The scale of the problem is now becoming much clearer, and the massive measures already taken have been appropriate in relation to the unfolding crisis. Actually we have more enemies within the capitalist tent than without these days.

Politically, with the collapse of communism and its command economy philosophy, there is no philosophy to rival 'free markets' internationally. But in the UK, the malcontents, who have never come to terms with that communist command economy collapse, and continue to resent the unequal prosperity of free markets, seem to have found a strong voice within the media.

These are clever people who know how to manipulate information, and slant emphasis, to maximise all of the adverse news.

Some of the economic commentary has been quite vicious in its innuendos, falling into the category of shouting 'Fire' in an overcrowded assembly. The BBC has not been immune from complicity. Carol Thatcher, apparently the symbol of free markets, is openly vilified and dumped, whilst Jonathan Ross bounces back from his latest misdemeanours.

There are of course socialist voices trying to reintroduce control from the top – the man in Whitehall knows best. This will hopefully be strongly resisted, as we know from experience he never does.

If Harriet Harman had any economic power, what few green shoots that did appear would be immediately suffocated by interference.

Gordon Brown of course is widely blamed now for the mess to which he undoubtedly contributed; but he is respected internationally for a powerful financial mind, even if he has misused it domestically. His efforts to synchronise a global response to what is not a UK-derived problem, but a worldwide one, have been and continue to be positive. It is sad for him that the massive transfer of resources out of the wealth-producing sector in the UK into the public one has not produced the shining public services he presumably hoped for, and what many of the continental economies enjoy already.

Whilst attention has been focused on petty blunders like 'Fred the Shred's' pension excesses (referring to Fred Goodwin, Royal Bank of Scotland chief executive), the general thrust of trying to get lending going, and trying to support small businesses is the important part. The main impacts of his policies are now where they should be, albeit anything done by government travels slowly through an obstacle course of bureaucracy.

Much criticism has centred on the argument that a crisis caused by excessive debt is not going to be solved by yet more debt. This misses the point. Whilst correct in the long term it is naive in the short term, as the current liquidity creation is merely replacing chunks of liquidity frozen in the banking system.

Clearly savings have got to rise, in particular in the Anglo-Saxon economies. By contrast, they have to fall somewhat in the over-saving Far Eastern economies, and Germany for that matter.

What is encouraging is the almost unanimous decisions of the leaders of the Far Eastern nations to use their large reserves aggressively to pump up demand and counteract the inevitable extra saving tendency of ordinary citizens of these countries, where there is no social safety net.

The credit splurge of the last five years has landed the western economies in their biggest potential recession since the war. The problem is large, but the coordinated actions of the world's free market leaders are on a grand scale too and highly positive. Keynes saw the need to emphasise the positive, since, as he said: 'Without spontaneous optimism economic activity does not revive.'

*Sterling*

It is easy to get carried away with one's convictions, but nobody is right for long about the future, particularly where currencies are concerned.

Having made a strong case for why sterling would have to fall against other currencies, the scale of the fall (about 30%) probably over-discounts the extent of the UK's specific problems on the short view.

Even in a sharp world downturn, the pound's fall is strongly stimulative and helpful to the UK economy. Effectively the UK is stealing the trade advantage by a competitive devaluation, and of course it is not popular with Britain's European partners. Already there are clear signs of its positive effect. Occupancy of Millennium and Copthorne Hotels in New York were off 40% in January; Beijing and Hong Kong were off 20%; and London a mere 4%. London is currently the most busy retail centre of any European city.

There is a near explosion of domestic bookings for the coming holiday season. Upwards of three quarters of a million might take their holidays in the UK instead of on the (now) Costa Too Mucha. That represents several billion pounds of spending in UK pubs, hotels, holiday lets and local shops, etc.

Whilst UK manufacturers are currently claiming a 12% fall in orders, when restocking returns (and the falling off a cliff of orders in the last quarter would have been primarily due to heavy destocking), British-based companies are now likely to get an above average share of orders going. The lower pound also helps the property collateral of the UK banks and building societies.

Property in the UK in hard currency terms is already down 50%. It won't fall so far in sterling terms, in which covenants and collateral are measured. By mid year the UK could be looking relatively more resilient than most other economies and this could lead to quite a sharp upward recovery in sterling – say to $1.6 and €1.25.


**Market and Currency Update – 2 April**
FTSE 100 – 3,955

Capitalism is going through one of its biggest crises in free market history. It's worth looking at its history, as the way out will lie in reaffirming its core benefits, but with a better understanding of the desirable checks and balances to keep the system on the rails.

The great ideological struggle of the twentieth century has been between collectivism and liberalism (the free market economy). Collectivism was defined 80 years ago by English jurist and constitutional theorist Albert Dicey as:

Government for the good of the people by experts or officials who know or think they know what is good for the people better than any non official person or than the mass of the people themselves.

It is now generally accepted that collectivism – the theory and practice of the collective ownership of land and the means of production, the state runs everything – has, where practised, been the biggest economic disaster of the twentieth century.

Historically there is no recorded example of any collectivist society ending other than in abject failure. In the twentieth century all collectivist societies except North Korea have already collapsed – though the current state of that economy hardly makes a compelling case for collectivism.

Frederick Hayek, the modern high priest of free markets and capitalism, maintained that such collapse was inevitable:

Prices, liberals would argue, are a better regulator of human energy than any centralised planning authority.

Keynes described the collectivist as: 'someone who wanted to replace private choice by government choice'. Karl Popper, philosopher and professor at The London School of Economics, rejected the 'planning society of Marxism', claiming that the future is open and follows no predetermined path. The future depends on how we behave. This certainly is very relevant to achieve our recovery from the present economic predicament.

Karl Popper believed it was impossible for the state to have the knowledge to undertake holistic planning. He maintained that 'attempts to remodel society end with planners being driven to transform human nature to fit their plans, rather than adapting their plans to fit human nature.'

Hayek argued that the planning authority lacked the information to solve the vast number of equations needed to coordinate the demand and supply of millions of products.

Adam Smith, the father of modern capitalism, insisted that the state should only raise revenue for its necessary functions: defence, law and order, and the provision of public goods needed to facilitate commerce in general.

The architect of the collectivist system, though he never lived to see it in operation, was Karl Marx. He claimed that capitalist accumulation took place by depriving workers of the fruits of their labour – and in this unjust remuneration mechanism lay the doom of the system. He also predicted that capitalism would collapse as a result of its own greed and corruption. Shades of our current troubles unfortunately.

The instability of the old Latin American dictatorships sprung from the inequity of 97% of the nations' wealth being held by 3% or less of the population. The republic of Bolivia has had 187 'military coups' in 188 years since independence, with little discernible improvement in GDP.

Modern capitalism is now anyway, as a result of that unfairness of income distribution in the late nineteenth and early twentieth centuries, a mixture of collectivism (state interference) and free markets.

In 1866 in the six leading industrial nations, the state's share of the economy was under 10%. By 1985 it had risen to 47%. This then proved to be a bridge too far in state control, as sclerosis set in, and a backlash occurred.

It was then that Ronald Reagan, along with Maggie Thatcher, began a crusade against the collectivist public sector, and set about rolling back the state. They provided the ideological drive and personal leadership which made anti-collectivism a cause, and paved the way for two decades of impressive wealth creation.

Reagan famously stated: 'In the present crisis government is not the solution to our problems, government is the problem.'

Perhaps Gordon Brown, as he saves the planet, could reflect on this. [*Brown, in a slip of the tongue in the Commons, had stated that he was trying to save the world.*]

Joseph Strumpeter, the Austrian economist (1883-1950) famously described capitalism as 'creative destruction'. The problem under communism was that the creativity was stifled by bureaucracy and regulation, but the destruction happened anyway. Communist countries still had the Trabant when the Morris Minor, its equivalent, had moved off the road into a motor museum.

According to Václav Klaus, the charismatic Czech leader:

The enduring question facing modern economies is the extent to which The State should be allowed to interfere with the freedom of the individual.

He strongly believes in this respect that Brussels has gone much too far. Red tape is estimated to cost British industry £77 billion a year. He has emphasised that under the current six-month Czech presidency of the EU, they will seek to free private enterprise from yet more controls as the best response to the current economic crisis.

Unfortunately, whenever capitalism runs into a crisis, and we are certainly in one now, all the crypto-collectivists come out of the woodwork and tend to dominate the airwaves.

Luckily for much of the UK population, financial news is a turn off and they switch to football. Otherwise the economy would have probably ground to a complete halt long ago.

It hasn't. At ordinary family level, a sensible effort to get their own balance sheets in better order has been taking place. Credit card debt is down, savings have risen, and all those on long-term variable rate mortgages are significantly better off.

Meanwhile the 30% devaluation of sterling has been a highly beneficial stimulus, undoubtedly at the expense of our trading partners. London is the only European city with retail sales rising. The housing market, which in continental and US currency terms has halved, is showing signs of picking up quite well.

With the approaching end of the viciously extreme des-tocking of October to January, commercial activity is thawing.

The authorities have done much more for the banks than the banks have so far done for their customers. The UK banks apparently are less accommodating than their continental counterparts. But great pressure is on them to loosen up.

All is not so gloomy as it was. Meanwhile, in the stock market there is a growing indication that sellers are getting exhausted.

Bull markets are born out of seller exhaustion, not buyer enthusiasm. The latter is where bear markets begin.

Steve Ballmer, head of Microsoft, said:

We are certainly in the midst of a once in a lifetime set of economic conditions. The perspective I would bring is not one of recession – rather that the economy is reset-ting at a lower level of business and consumer spending based largely on the reduced leverage in the economy.

This certainly goes for the Anglo-Saxon economies, but the process is well on its way. By contrast, Asia and Latin America are significantly under-leveraged; Chile has no net government debt, and both a current account and budget surplus. Likewise Hong Kong, Singapore and China. They must help by stepping into the breach, but at least they are capable of it.

Not all is as black as the media would have us believe. The free spirit of capitalism is beginning to work its way through this crisis.

## Market and Currency Update – 1 May
FTSE 100 – 4,390 (5 May)

*The stock market*

From where markets are now there seem to be a number of different possible outcomes:

1.  Most markets have now got back to near their 200-day moving averages. They are thus facing strong resistance levels technically. The large rise from 3,500

to 4,400 has also made the markets technically over-bought. Wall Street is up from 6,700 to 8,400.

2. There still remain almost overwhelming amounts of cash sitting on the sidelines, mesmerised into inactivity by the last 12 months of fearsome volatility. Now, fear of missing out could start to move it. Also solvency ratios will have improved for institutions, which will enable them to allocate more to equities.

3. The savage destocking of Oct/Feb almost worldwide is out of the way so orders will pick up somewhat, but western consumers cannot go back to their debt habit of the last decade. So consumption will not return to previous levels; that is, until new wealth is created to enable it. That takes time.

4. The economies that could expand their domestic consumption – those economies holding the surplus side of the debts run up by the overspending West – have got to do so.

With regard to the latter point, there are question marks over this. The populations of these economies are primarily compulsive savers, particularly the Chinese and the Germans. Habits of a lifetime don't change overnight – so moving from saving to spending will in the first instance have to be done by their governments. The Chinese seem to have accepted this better than the Germans, though in their predominantly command economy the institutions by which it can be done are weak. Japan has been trying to make its compulsive savers spend for a decade without much effect.

The rebalancing of the world economy that now has to take place looks as if it will face a number of obstacles before it is achieved. But it must be achieved, before genuine world growth can resume. There remain a huge number of uncertainties out there, but the worst should hopefully be behind us.

## Market and Currency Update – 1 June
FTSE 100 – 4,418 (29 May)

*Investment outlook*

We are in a world of experiment. Never before has about 5% of world GDP been hurled into the world economy by collective governmental action to stimulate it. Never before has the banking system entered a recession with reserves that have been decimated because a portion was invested in toxic assets of dubious value, and added to this the banks face the usual write-downs on their normal loan books as the recession unrolls.

Never before, except in wartime, have any major economic blocks run government deficits, which this year in the UK and USA will reach about 12% of GDP.

Nobody frankly knows how all these new known unknowns are actually going to work out. However, it is almost inevitable that such a massive monetary stimulus will lead to a recovery of sorts, at the very least.

In the first instance, the created liquidity tends to feed much more quickly into stock markets than the underlying economies. Hence the sharp recovery we have seen in markets since the March low.

Other home truths might be that we are now in a world where no leading currency looks particularly attractive, as the printing presses whirl at a record rate everywhere. So the conditions for gold look more favourable than in previous recessions.

According to Merrill Lynch we may be in year 9 of an 18-year secular bear market such as the 1966 to 1982 market. In that instance, the place to be was equities because inflation wiped out 70% of the value of bonds. War Loan fell from nearly par to a mere 35% of its face value at one point. Those who held bonds or, worse still, long-dated government

194

securities, lost most of their wealth. Equities fared far better. There was no overall real growth but they preserved their purchasing power. Skilful equity fund managers made huge real returns in this generally static market by exploiting the considerable ups and downs or by choosing the well run companies that outperformed.

Merrill Lynch also points out that (short term) all three indicators that have never failed in the past to signal the end of a cyclical bear market in equities, and in the economy, have turned positive since Christmas: the Institute for Supply Chain Management (ISM) Manufacturing Index; the Conference Board coincident-to-lagging indicator ratio; and the University of Michigan Consumer Sentiment Index.

The ISM Manufacturing Index bottomed in December 2008 at 32.9 (now 40). The Conference Board's coincident-to-lagging ratio has just turned in three successive lows. Data going back to 1960 showed recessions ended within two months of this event.

The University of Michigan Consumer Sentiment Index bottomed in November at 55 and is now at 65. Typically recessions end within six months of this lagging indicator.

In stock market terms at the very least it has become dangerous to be short of the market.

## Market and Currency Update – 1 July
FTSE 100 – 4,250 (3 Jul)

*Equities*

Markets everywhere have rallied strongly from their March lows when the index in the UK hit 3,500, but resistance was bound to be met as they nearly all recovered from deeply oversold positions to their 200-day moving average level. In order for a new bull market to occur this level has to be decisively breached on the upside.

Markets exhaust themselves by very big rises. The sheer size of the recovery needed from the March lows to get back to the long-term 200-day moving average line would at the least suggest that there would be insufficient energy left to make the breach upwards as well. This is what seems to be happening, and markets now appear to be in consolidation mode.

However, taking the longer-term view, I am just going to quote here what Warren Buffet said back in October 2008 (when markets were just about reaching the same low as March 2009):

> The financial world is in a mess, both in the United States and abroad. Its problems, moreover, have been leaking into the general economy, and the leaks are now turning into a gusher. In the near term unemployment will rise, business activity will falter, and the headlines will continue to be scary. So I've been buying American stocks. This is for my personal account, in which previously I held 100% bonds. My net worth will soon be 100% in US equities.

He goes on:

> WHY? To be sure investors are right to be wary of highly leveraged entities or businesses in weak competitive positions. But fears regarding the long-term prosperity of the nation's many sound companies makes no sense. These businesses will indeed suffer earnings hiccups, as they always have, but most major companies will be setting new profit records 5, 10, and 20 years from now.

Let me be clear on one point. I can't predict short term movements of the stock market. What is likely however is the market will move higher, perhaps substantially so, well before sentiment or the economy turns up.

Equities will almost certainly outperform cash over the next decade, probably by a substantial degree.

**Market and Currency Update – August**
FTSE 100 – 4,755 (13 Aug)

Market analyst David Buick (of BGC Partners) announced on Bloomberg (business and financial news network and online forum) this morning that everybody who is anybody in the City is away on holiday now and only 'The Brain Dead' are left behind.

As one of the latter, I am reassured by a feeling I have had for years that 'The Brains' in the City are often the source of its problems. Indeed there are times when the capacity of their 'brains' appear to be in inverse proportion to the amount of common sense they possess. These 'starred firsts', with their feet firmly planted in mid air, rush headlong into every bubble – the bankers have a special flair for this – and are usually the first to panic.

Such conduct would turn every economic set-back into a calamity were it not for the 'stupid people'. They turn off the bad news, switch to watching sport, and get on with life as best they can. Thus economic meltdown is averted.

Anyway, the 'brain dead' haven't been doing too badly recently. In spite of looking already over-bought by the 10% rise in July, the market keeps going on up.

There is no doubt that by historical standards there is still a vast amount of money sitting on the sidelines with no prospect of getting any decent return from cash holdings. So any substantial or even minor setback is likely to see more of this money moving back into equities.

In recent months corporate bonds have been the principal beneficiary of this cash mountain. Perceived to be less risky than equities, they have attracted the lion's share, and all the higher yielding corporate bonds have put in a stellar performance over the last six months. Some of the more risky financial bonds have doubled, and the corporate bonds of cyclical companies like BMW, GKN, Lafarge, etc. have shown 10–20% appreciation since their launch, as well as a good running yield of frequently more than 7%.

A lot of these bonds are now looking fairly fully valued with little or no protection at these higher levels against a resurgence of inflation. So it is not surprising that more money is moving towards equities, which are seen as a long-term inflation-proof asset.

Another perverse factor is the very wrong pro-cyclicality of bank, pension fund and insurance regulation, and new accountancy rules. This virtually means they cannot buy when stock markets are low and their collateral values have fallen, but after the market has risen substantially the recovery of collateral values enables them to buy more equities again. This is exacerbated by 'mark to market' accountancy where, as the iconic head of AXA, Henri de Castries, pointed out after the Lehman collapse: 'If a forced seller leads to one house in a street selling at a very low price it is ridiculous to value every other house in the street at that distressed sale value.' But this is precisely what 'mark to market' forces on them.

So in the UK a few distressed sales in the property market in 2008 led to virtually the entire UK quoted property sector becoming technically insolvent.

It is just as pro-cyclical (i.e. makes the cycle worse in both directions) in a booming market. Illiquid stocks rise to great heights and then large holdings of big institutions are marked to market, though no way could such large chunks ever sell at anything like the marginal inflated price. But apparent collateral soars, so greater debt can be taken on.

There will have to be changes to this valuation method.

So with markets now back to near pre-Lehman levels there is more institutional capacity to buy. That does not automatically mean that they will use it. But it does mean it is a potential added prop to the recovery.


**Market and Currency Update – September**
FTSE 100 – 4,930 (7 Sep)

It is not difficult to see what Gordon Brown's strategy is to try to win the next election. He knows he has no hope if unemployment is still rising and the economy remains depressed. So he will try to manipulate the economy with government (created) money so that he can go to the polls on the twin ticket as follows: 'I saved the world' (he has credited himself with that already) and 'I have now saved the UK economy'.

The clear 'Brown' policy for the UK is to leave the bloated public sector totally untouched – not a single person will lose their job before the election. And the government will borrow what it takes to bring forward and maximize all possible public construction works in the next 12 months.

If this leads to weaker sterling then so be it as that will help jobs too by encouraging tourism in the UK, and promoting exports.

On the international front, as he has been doing at the G20 meeting, Gordon Brown will encourage all countries to run large government deficits for at least the next 12 months so that Britain doesn't look like the odd man out. That would bring an uncomfortable spotlight on sterling's credibility.

If that led to a sterling crisis Brown's Ponzi scheme (a

fraudulent investment operation, coined after the infamous Charles Ponzi scam) would blow up in his face. It is not surprising that quantitative easing is going flat out in the UK, as it effectively mops up the massive gilt sales the government has to make to cover its ballooning deficit. These would otherwise almost certainly not be covered by genuine demand.

This is a high risk strategy but must appeal to someone who is clearly in a political last chance saloon. Frankly Brown's strategy will be a close run thing as the more perceptive financial commentators are already drawing attention to the fallacy of such a risky financial course.

Liam Halligan, in a recent *Daily Telegraph* article entitled 'Britain sleepwalking towards a decade of economic misery', highlighted that these policies are digging us into an even greater hole. He writes:

> Any beneficial impact of our wildly expansionary fiscal and monetary stance will soon be over. Once the sugar rush fades asset prices will start reflecting the far more significant downsides of the UK reckless policy of printing money and racking up ever more government debt.

If Brown's wheeze is successful, however, the cold winter will actually be delayed until post-May election 2010. Brown has basically got to fool 'enough of the people, enough of the time' to get away with it until next May. I am not saying he won't. After all, a joke going round the Internet at the moment pays tribute to his mental agility with the truth. It goes as follows:

Brown has finally resigned, and the Cabinet want to give him a leaving present by which he will be remembered. They agree to name a steam engine after him. So they go to the York Steam Museum to find a suitable choice. However, the curator states that all that is left are a few freight engines and the odd shunting engine, and a new name-plate would be very expensive to make anyway.

So due to the credit crunch they ask if he can think of anything cheaper.

'Yes,' he says, 'we could simply paint out the "F" of *The Flying Scotsman*.'

August has seen a further quite strong rise in world markets, building on the already strong latter half of July. We are now back to pre-Lehman levels almost everywhere, and Hong Kong – a bellwether for the Far East – is again at 20,000 from 12,000 last November.

Ignoring the possibly freak peak of 25,000 in early 2008, 20,000 does represent a fairly distinct double top, and certainly a relatively stiff resistance level. But most markets have broken up above their 200-day moving averages, and that in general is the sign of a bull market.

Whilst the market generally now looks over-bought after this long and strong rise, the level of uncommitted funds suggests that any set-back – in the absence of very poor economic news – will not be that large. But world growth must by definition be held back for some years compared to the previous rates.

The necessary repayment of the previously created excess credits will determine this. We should expect staid earnings performances for some time to come, with a much higher differential between the skilfully managed and the also-ran companies in every sector.

We are now really moving to a market of stocks rather than a one-way stock market.

## Market and Currency Update – October
FTSE 100 – 5,154 (8 Oct)

Looking through my old newsletters, I came across an interesting quote by Lord Hanson in 1991. He said:

> If ever a Labour government gets back into power the UK gilt market will become the biggest junk bond market in the world.

A decade of Labour government on and his prediction might be close to being fulfilled.

It looks as if the pension funds, which have been encouraged to put more money in gilts, and have unwisely done so, will then be declaring very dismal money pensions in 10 or 20 years time for their subscribers.

What explains the worldwide boom in stock markets since March? The British market is now a small tail wagged by the much larger dog of Asia and the US, as most of the companies of the FTSE 100 are worldwide operations with little exposure to the UK's particular problems.

Markets have responded to the realisation that a complete financial meltdown has passed. It looked more than possible after the Lehman collapse exposed the full rottenness of the banking edifice. We are back in a recognisable cyclical recession. One thing everybody knows about them is that eventually they will reverse. Investors perhaps feel comfortable with the familiarity of that.

It might be, however, that perception of the timing of the recovery is too optimistic. What is certain is that the bargains have gone; one now has to tread much more carefully.

## Market and Currency Update – November
FTSE 100 – 5,142 (6 Nov)

It is worth remembering that in May 2006 the FTSE 100 index was at 6,025. So we are still a long way from the position nearly four years ago in spite of the recent recovery, and that is in nominal terms, not real terms. But of course since then the dislocation of the world economy has happened and a lot of wealth destruction has occurred.

By contrast, China, India, Asia, and countries like Brazil, have made real progress in the development of their underlying economies over this period.

In December last year I wrote a paper on 'What is the likelihood of a sterling crisis in 2009?', starting with the question: 'Who will bail out the bailer-outers?' There is no Marshall Plan around this time. The answer was no one – other than ourselves. So another £30 billion hurled into the UK banks last week (probably a necessary measure but hardly instantly wealth creating) just adds to the burden.

The other main point of my paper was that those countries that used the extra borrowing they were taking on most productively and creatively would put themselves into the economic recovery mode first. Last autumn's mini budget was described by Simon Heffer (*Telegraph* columnist) as follows:

> It was an aggressively sectarian set of measures. Labour has identified its people – the client state of public sector bureaucrats, operatives, and claimants, sedulously created by Brown since 1997, and the autumn budget's main purpose was to protect them.

Since then, our 'Cash for Clunkers' programme has primarily helped the Korean economy. Hyundai's small cheap car imports to the UK have surged, as have the small Renaults, made in Slovenia. By contrast, the similar schemes of Germany, France and the US have benefited their own domestic car industries by at least 80%.

Gerard Lyons, chief economist of Standard Chartered Bank, states:

> I have been struck by how different the debate is here to other parts of the world; because of the depth of the recession, the focus in the UK has been on the size of the public debt and the quantity of govt spending. In contrast there is more focus in Asia on the quality of govt spending. It's not about boosting the economy now but positioning it for the future.

Lyons then gives examples:

> In South Korea (world's No. 12 economy) the govt stimulus has gone into tax cuts and infrastructure spending, but an essential focus is on positioning the economy as a global leader in fusion and green energy. In China, the huge stimulus – and they could afford it – has gone into domestic infrastructure and they have unveiled 20 new industry funds to seed more investment away from old industries to new sectors such as environment, software, and IT.

He goes on to point out that 'growth is the best way to reduce the UK budget deficit' and that the UK 'needs to create, like successful economies elsewhere, the right hard infrastructure (such as road and rail) and soft infrastructure, boosting skills and education.'

A study for the Business Council of England demonstrated that the UK was 24th out of 27 countries on infrastructure (France was 4th), and that excluded China. Equally damaging is the comparison by the OECD (Organisation for

Economic Co-Operation and Development) on research & development spending: with Finland at 3.5%, Germany and the US at 2.6%, Japan at 3.4%, and the UK at 1.8% of GDP.

Anecdotal evidence indicates that current government priorities continue to favour the non-productive sector; and tightening on any infrastructure spend such as reducing the water companies' future infrastructure budgets, cutting defence expenditure (except where there is a huge media outcry), and, according to the construction industry, cutting government contracts, not increasing them.

The new government after May must concentrate on increasing capital expenditure projects, but cutting sharply expenditure on 'paper shifters' and 'committee sitters', who produce no real work for anybody else, and leave nothing to show for it.

Meanwhile the increasingly intrusive agencies of this government seem to proliferate so that the feeling one gets is not far from how nineteenth-century French anarchist Pierre-Joseph Proudhon described the behaviour of governments in his time:

To be governed is to be watched, inspected, spied on, regulated, indoctrinated, controlled, ruled and censored by persons who have neither wisdom nor virtue.

Under pretext of the public good it is to be exploited, embezzled, robbed, and then at the least protest, fined, harassed, vilified, bludgeoned, imprisoned, shot or garrotted.

As to the stock market, it is important to remember that the FTSE 100 is composed principally of companies with little or no UK business. After the large and almost non-stop rise from March, apart from the July blip, everybody sees markets as being too high and ripe for a reaction. Markets don't do what people expect for the simple reason that what everybody expects is already discounted.

## Market and Currency Update – December
FTSE 100 – 5,286 (15 Dec)

It's official – the UK is now a Third World state. After ten years of Gordon Brown's economic stewardship, Britain is now 14th out of 16 European nations in terms of providing cancer therapy. You are likely to get better treatment everywhere else with the possible exception of Latvia and Bulgaria. Yet some of the most advanced science in the world in cancer research is occurring in Britain.

Britain's railways now have the lowest punctuality record of any of the European countries; even including those on the far side of the old Berlin Wall. No Mussolini in sight either to make them run on time. A Swiss tourist was recently reported to have had a heart attack when three of his four connections had been missed, due to 'late running' trains. His Swiss constitution could not accommodate such an alien concept.

More disturbing has been the systemic attempt to undermine the very structure of British society – the family – by this government. The chief executive of a new quango, Dr Rake, the Family Equality and Fairness Commission, devoted its first paper to rubbishing the 'natural' family, and suggested that children nowadays were just as well off being brought up by a variety of relations – uncles, aunts and any other members of the extended family – but not necessarily the mother and father together. She warned politicians 'not to encourage traditional families'.

On closer scrutiny, it emerged that one of the 'trustees' of this quango was none other than Alastair Campbell's 'partner'. Such is the depth of cronyism in the public sector.

The problem is that under this government there has been

creeping 'statism' promoted under the bogus fronts of fairness, equality and safety.

As Professor Mancur Olson stated in his *Rise and Decline of Nations*:

> The history of the rise and fall of collectivism shows that people want security as well as freedom, and it is all too easy for idealists, intellectuals and scoundrels to force populations into an iron cage of bondage in the name of providing security against real or imagined ills.

In fact by the systemic manipulation of data, information and ideas, those people who believe (but daren't say it openly) that 'the state' knows best and is superior to the 'individual' can restrict the freedom of the individual, and of course consequently increase the power of state officials.

Harriet Harman, after crashing into somebody's parked car while allegedly on her mobile phone, recently said in defence of not having given her name and address: 'Everybody knows who I am and where to find me.' She is not 'HH', the individual under the law, but Harriet Harman, part of the state – in her eyes she *is* the law.

One of the economic consequences of this pseudo-communist endeavour to control our lives has been an inevitable expansion in the number of public sector employees required to police the growing raft of regulations.

Irwin Stelzer, a well-known economic commentator, is well aware of the severe damage this has done to the UK balance sheet and says that in order to reverse this: 'The Tory leader must act tougher than the Iron Lady – or else 'be the prime minister who let the IMF do his dirty work.'

Reversing this public sector growth, a lot of which is now embedded in legislation, looks like a bigger task than curbing the excessive powers of the unions, which faced Margaret Thatcher.

# 16

## *2010*

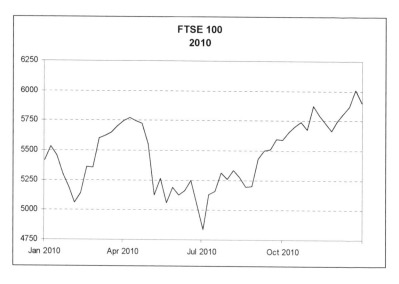

**Figure 45**

*[The year 2010 started off with the FTSE 100 index comfortably above 5,000. There had also been an enormous recovery in bond markets, particularly the corporate bonds of financial institutions. This had been particularly marked in the financial sector of the market where fears at the beginning of the year of default now looked remote, with the enormous support the sector had received both from governments and central banks.*

208

*Far Eastern and other strong emerging markets, such as Brazil and India, had given a stellar performance in 2009 and entered 2010 in an atmosphere of further high hope. There was still enormous risk aversion around in European investment circles, with commentators focusing on many real ongoing problems as well as plenty of imaginary ones. Because of risk aversion, the focus of equity investment had stayed on large and mega companies, but there were still plenty of bargains among smaller companies where the 'fearful' feared to tread.*]

## Market and Currency Update – February
FTSE 100 – 5,184

*Why neither Greece, nor for that matter any of the other 'PIIGS' (Portugal, Italy, Ireland, Greece and Spain), will cause the collapse of the euro.*

The British press and media, along with the politicians of all parties, have demonstrated once again how the British do not understand how Europe thinks or operates. The British are outside their culture. This is why the UK has never sat comfortably within the European Union and why it has been the least competent country at exploiting its benefits.

But actually our perverse civil service, itself culturally euro-supercilious, has made an absolute mare's nest of formulating the UK versions of all EU legislation. This has been to the profound detriment of British industry, and agriculture in particular. Britain has deliberately shackled itself by bureaucratic gold-plating.

The rest of Europe flouts the regulations to apply them with very stretchy elasticity indeed, inconveniencing themselves as little as possible. This has cost the UK billions over the period.

The attitude of the British medical professional is a perfect example of this cultural mismatch. The president of the BMA wrote a letter to *The Guardian* last week expressing outrage at the error of a German doctor parachuted in to carry out off-duty services for British GPs who, alone of all European GPs, put their feet up promptly at 5pm every day, necessitating external cover for 77.2% of the 24/7 week. (Of course illness does not confine itself to working hours.)

The letter stated that 'foreign' doctors should have to come 'up' to the standards of the British medical professional before being allowed to practise in the UK.

Is he not aware that the record of British medicine is now so poor in the European context that the UK lies 14th out of 16 EU countries in terms of medical performance?

That same day, whilst carrying this letter, which decried the German's single drug blunder and implied that a British-trained doctor would never have made a mistake like that, the same newspaper published an article stating that the NHS was paying out more than £60 million in compensation to no less than 100 young children who had all been wrongly diagnosed with epilepsy and had been given powerful drugs that had permanently damaged their lives. The drugs were administered by a very senior (British) consultant, and it turned out that not one of these children had epilepsy.

Returning to the euro collapse scenario, firstly one has to imagine what would have happened in this monster world-wide financial meltdown if the euro had not existed. There would have been immediate speculative routs on virtually all the smaller European currencies of the countries that are now safely under the euro umbrella. These countries know that, and are aware of the mayhem it would have caused them.

The euro has created an area of immense financial stability with a hugely powerful and credible central bank backed by immense reserves. The short-term pain of staying within the single currency, for these countries that have conducted their fiscal policy irresponsibly, may be quite high. But it is nothing compared to the devastation and the speed of the enforced retrenchment they would face outside and alone. Nobody, who is in it, is going to leave the euro.

The problems of Greece, which represents just 2% of EU GDP, are similar to Britain having a little local trouble in Cornwall. Portugal's GDP is less than the turnover of Microsoft. As to Spain, firstly the Spaniards are no soft Latinos. Spaniards do not historically renege on their debts. Spanish fiscal policy was a model of orthodoxy with a 2% budget surplus prior to the world crash. They have powerful interests and strong investments throughout prosperous Latin America to call on.

Twenty-five per cent of Italy's economy is undeclared, so the official figures look far worse than the much stronger reality. Real debt to GDP is not 100% but about 75%.

The euro was anyway overvalued versus the entire dollar area, which of course includes China and Asia, so the recent 11% rise of the dollar against the euro will help Europe significantly. It may need to go further. It is a necessary and beneficial rebalancing of the EU/Asian/US competitive position.

But reading the British press in the past few days, one would be led to believe that the EU and its euro 'experiment' was about to disintegrate. There is only grief for the British in the disintegration of the euro and the very considerable economic dislocation associated with such an outcome. Britain's prosperity is intricately linked with that of Europe, and a prosperous and stable Europe is the UK's greatest possible self-interest.

*General outlook – April 2010*

The world seems to be separating into two different divisions, the second of which also has to be subdivided:

Division 1: Those nations with low borrowings, high savings and, as a result, a strong national balance sheet with a balance of payments surplus.

Division 2: Those countries with high borrowings, low savings and what might be described as a very weak balance sheet with too much debt. These countries have to be subdivided into two categories:

A. Those that are tackling this problem with imagination and vigour (Ireland for instance – 5% salary cut throughout the public sector).

B. Those that appear to lack the political will to do so, or are taking the least effective steps to improve their national balance sheet (i.e. supporting their economies with borrowed money in the wrong way.)

Clearly the countries in the first category are: China, Hong Kong, Singapore, Taiwan, Malaysia, India, Korea, New Zealand, and possibly Australia – although personal borrowing is high in the latter. Then emerging economies like Brazil and Chile; and of the old economies, Canada, Norway, Germany, Holland, Sweden, France (just) and Japan (always a bit of an enigma but certainly an efficient economy with hard-working, clever people).

In the second division – category A – we have, arguably, the USA, most Eastern European countries with a question mark over Hungary (as usual – high propensity to overspend at state level), and Spain. Also, probably Italy – it always extricates itself somehow and has very high domestic savings.

In the second division – category B – I regrettably have to put the UK where now, thanks to a decade of Labour feathering its own constituency, a thoroughly bloated public sector continues to be sheltered (from the need to bring about an immediate reduction and efficiency reform) behind the mantra: 'Don't let a deficit reduction undermine the recovery.'

So the nation is encouraged to go on living in a world of make-believe, where you could describe the whole programme of public support for the economy as: 'One gigantic exercise in economic illusion.' This continues to weaken the economy further. This is also very unfair on the many valuable people who work tirelessly in the public sector, ever more hampered by swaths of job-creating bureaucracy.

The reluctance to tackle this glaring problem within the British economy has already resulted in the exchange rate of sterling falling 25% in the last 15 months, both against the euro and the dollar. Part of that was an adjustment to previously overvalued sterling, but more than half would be accounted for by the international community's perception that Britain is showing a marked reluctance to face reality.

Possibly, for political reasons ahead of the election, the opposition has shown little resolution to taking the necessary axe to the bloated part of the public sector too. Failing to give clear leadership in the economic arena has backfired. The Conservatives have made themselves look no more credible than Labour.

Clearly if the present government returns, should the electorate swallow its tapestry of lies, sterling will go on going down until there is a sterling crisis and the IMF turns up.

If the Tories win, sterling could rally strongly; as long as they do display vigorous determination and enact the right measures to rebalance the economy away from the state and back to the productive sector. If they shy away from tackling the public sector then sterling will continue to be undermined.

The investment consequences of the above indicate that future equity growth (for the same starting level in price earnings terms) will be in the Far East and first category of economies. Then the USA, with its enormous turnaround potential, looks the next most promising area. Bear in mind that many US companies are multinationals with significant emerging market exposure or strong exporters to Asia and other emerging markets.

Europe is rather a mixed bag of opportunities and, like the UK, is weighed down in general by relatively hefty welfare and state overheads. But unlike the UK, it can boast an almost universally superb infrastructure and a first-class public health service.

In company terms Europe has a significant number of powerful and well-established multinationals operating in the fastest growing markets in the world. In France, companies like LVMH, L'Oreal, Michelin, Air Liquide, Ciments Français, Lafarge, Alsthom; in Germany, Volkswagen (now China's largest motor company), Siemens, BASF, Bayer, BMW, Daimler, etc.; and of course the Swiss multinationals – Nestlé, Novartis, Roche, Syngenta and the rest.

When it comes to the FTSE 100, if you exclude the UK utilities, nearly 80% of its earnings are derived outside British shores. So the UK economy could collapse, whilst the FTSE 100 could easily hit new highs. As it is priced in sterling, the index is nothing like as high as it appears. At the present exchange rate, it is equivalent to about 4,800 in Swiss francs, dollars or euros.

Going forward, the big risk to UK investors must be UK fixed interest securities, and sterling cash balances. That having been said, the current depressed level of sterling has already built in the government's failures to date! If political change leads to better economic management, sterling could recover substantially. Markets are much more skilful discount mechanisms than measurers of value. The present value of sterling discounts a gloomy outcome, because what has been written above is easy enough for everybody to see.

Bill Gross, the very successful manager of the world's largest bond fund, PIMCO, recently stated that: 'UK gilts were sitting on a bed of nitroglycerine.'

Last year UK corporate bonds started from a very high

214

yield level so in many cases the capital appreciation of those bonds has completely compensated investors for being in a depreciating currency. We cannot expect that to happen next year. If anything, yields might start to rise, and capital appreciation will be replaced by capital losses.

Furthermore, the gilt market has been artificially upheld by quantitative easing and regulatory-driven demand from UK pension funds, which defies any financial logic. These artificial props cannot last.

## Market and Currency Update – May
FTSE 100 – 5,304

There is certainly plenty to comment on since the March newsletter. Paul Volcker made an interesting observation on finance and bank reform:

> I wish someone would give me one shred of neutral evidence that financial innovation has led to economic growth – one shred of evidence.

I recently met a mathematician who is now an honorary professor at the University of St Andrews. In 2006 he retired from a 20-year career at Lehman Brothers, constructing sophisticated financial derivatives for them to sell to their clients. He stated that he would never have bought any of the derivatives he had constructed. All these products are a zero sum game – i.e. one man's gain is another's loss. The only winner every time is the casino owner (in this case the investment bank) who takes a cut from both sides of the transaction each time it happens. These are skillfully sold to gullible corporate treasurers, using the new weasel word that has recently entered the financial lexicon: 'DE-RISK'.

Any casino owner will tell you that his profit depends not on the behaviour of the gambling tables but on 'The Drop', i.e. the number of transactions that take place. The financial industry has enormous self-interest in promoting the use of them.

Every year, since the development of derivatives, the US and European corporate sectors ritually hand over billions of dollars of shareholders' profits to Wall Street and its side-kicks in London. They call it de-risking. Invariably the cost is many times higher than the risk.

This is of course concealed in 'footnotes' to company accounts. There 'the cash loss' is usually described as a 'foreign exchange adjustment' or 'an interest rate guarantee'. This is taken above the line, as it is not considered part of normal trading, and also so as not to compromise the trading profit figure (upon which bonuses may depend).

But the hard cash has gone out of the company and usually into the hands of the 'trader' or banker that advised the deal. They do these things every day and tend, by definition, to be better at it than company finance directors, who do it as a one-off or just occasionally and invariably get it wrong.

Mitchells & Butlers can tell us all about this. They blew a cool £250 million de-risking a potential interest rate exposure on a projected loan they never needed anyway, as the property deal envisaged did not happen.

Most recently The Prudential took out foreign exchange 'cover' on $21 billion of its potential deal to take over AIG Asia. The deal was then scrapped and, lo and behold, to close the position now no longer needed cost them a cool $450 million. This is the price of de-risking!

It poses a particular problem for the City, which makes or made a lot of money for 'UK PLC' out of other countries' economies. Much of the wider European financial business of this kind takes place in London. They walk into our casino. But the morality has a bad odour.

As Volcker clearly believes, this activity for economies generally is completely parasitic, and wealth reducing.

*The new government*

It is very early days to predict anything about the formal and surprising (from a UK political perspective) formation of the Tory-Lib Dem pact.

They start off with one great benefit – the cessation of the ongoing damage of Gordon Brown's economic management. His argument that the economy is still too fragile to risk making 'cuts' was holed below the waterline even before it was announced. Continuing to feed an alcoholic more alcohol, for fear of the trauma of detoxification, adds to the problem, not to the solution.

At last we can now live in hope rather than despair. Markets here should start to reflect this in due course, remembering that the FTSE 100 has little to do with the UK economy other than that the shares are valued in sterling. This makes them cheaper by the day and suggests the current level both of sterling and the market will not last long.

**Market and Currency Update – July**
FTSE 100 – 4,840

I am afraid the regularity of this former monthly newsletter has become the victim of regulation. The FSA, no doubt to avert attention from the scandalous failure of its banking supervision from 2005 onwards, has redoubled the regulatory framework and box-ticking culture for all areas remaining in its charge. This seems to have particularly homed in on retail fund management and private client investment management. So burdensome is the extra paperwork involved in every deal one does that the industry is literally being driven to 'collectives only', and standard asset allocations for everybody.

People want personalised management, but if the FSA has

anything to do with it, they will no longer get it. The FSA has made it too time consuming to be economic. So firms will simply bundle their clients into ranges of products pre-picked for each risk category into which the client 'fits'. Indeed the banks' wealth management services have done this already.

I have no intention of suddenly going down this barren route – albeit certain collectives can be very helpful for a good portfolio spread, and are probably best for small portfolios. Anyway, the net result is that the newsletter, which is time-consuming to write, will come less often in order to release time for 'KYC' (know your client) and 'Suitability' and 'File Notes'. These are obligatory to justify each time a transaction, however minor, occurs. Even if the decision is idiotic, provided it has been filed, suitability stamped, and KYC'd, my backside and the firm's is covered against the notorious 'arrow' inspections by the regulator.

Little do they seem to grasp that principles cannot be enforced by regulation. Actually regulation can drive out principle.

With regard to stock markets, fears of a 'second dip recession' don't frankly seem out of place, and – after a nearly 1,000 point drop in the FTSE 100 index – are probably reflected in the price anyway.

Over-borrowed economies like the UK's have got to rein in excessive government expenditure – if £60 billion or so is taken out of the spending, a lot of local businesses are going to get fewer sales.

Milton Friedman won his Nobel Prize for economics for demonstrating that one government-created job potentially destroyed two wealth-creating jobs. Reverse this process and in due course the economy will create more wealth, not less, and will consequently recover.

But there is no such negative pressure on the Far Eastern economies, nor Brazil, nor India. Europe is a mixture of highly indebted and lowly indebted. That the Germans, who are in the latter category, are hardly helping the over-indebted by screwing down their own expenditure, when they really don't need to, is disappointing.

There is an abundance of good value around at the moment.

[*July turned out to be a wonderful second chance for those who were out of the market to get in at a very attractive level. The 1,000-point fall since April had been completely made up by November.*]

# Conclusion

I am hesitant to use the word conclusion as it implies a finite outcome. In this brief decade we have seen almost everything: euphoria, wild panic, a normal cyclical recession and a massive financial collapse. We have seen a flight to sovereign bonds, a flight to alternative investments, a flight to property and a flight to hedge funds, culminating in the biggest financial 'Ponzi' ever – Madoff; plus a flight to gold.

A viewer from outer space would have to ask whether someone had let the lunatics out of the asylum to run our capital markets.

Looking down from on high on the world economy throughout this period, there was nothing to indicate an era of such wild fluctuations in financial performance. The world economy had progressed in nearly every corner of the globe more positively than during almost any previous decade in its history. Yet this decade saw the biggest financial meltdown for nearly a hundred years.

The defining event of this decade has been the effective collapse of the western financial system, which, but for some quick thinking by a handful of very able central bankers, could have brought the capitalist system to its knees, as happened after 1929.

That tragedy led to the prolonged impoverishment of very large numbers of honest, hard-working individuals world-wide through no fault of their own. Out of their despair rose many vengeful and more damaging forms of authoritarian regime. An economic background of despair and hopelessness becomes a fertile breeding ground for violence.

So a correct analysis of what went wrong and how to build a more solid framework in which the future financial system will operate is crucial. This cannot be done by the same generals that lost the previous battles. Wall Street will never reform Wall Street.

Since the investment bankers got their hands on other people's money after the repeal of Glass-Steagall, there seemed no limit to the excesses.

Previously failed regulators cannot possess the intellectual flexibility and imagination to define the new framework.

A lack of principles and a lack of ethical dimension to financial decision making look to be at the heart of the problem of why the system failed in the first place. Paul Krugman, the Nobel Prize-winning economist, stated:

The government needs to codify principles-based, not rule-based policies. This would, among other things, make it harder for the financial industry with its very good lawyers to find ways to evade legislative intent.

In this context, a letter recently published in the *Daily Telegraph* by the chief executive of the Institute of Chartered Accountants in England and Wales, Michael Izza, is relevant. He wrote:

Hector Sants, the chief executive of the FSA, questions whether principles-based regulation works for participants who have no principles. Principles-based regulation should not be confused with light touch regulation. Compliance with principles can be more demanding than applying rules, and in contrast to rules, a good set of principles focuses on substance rather than legal form.

We do not agree that a principles- based system depends upon the moral principles of the individuals within the system. Compared with box- ticking compliance with rules, principles generally offer a more effective check on unethical and immoral behaviour.

The best ideas often come from where one is least expecting them, because a new situation challenges a conventional approach to an issue. It requires fresh thinking from outside the existing tent.

We need fresh minds to re-engineer the new regulatory framework.

Those who produced the wealth in this decade did, arguably, an exceptional job. The financial sector, which supplied the oil for the engine of wealth to turn smoothly, ended up by flooding it, then running it almost dry, and nearly seizing it up. The failure of the financial markets has a lot to answer for to the rest of society. They were dealt the best hand in generations and spectacularly threw it away.

Since financial businesses attract allegedly all the cleverest graduates, because they pay the highest, what does this say about the usefulness of people with too much brain power? Is an excess of IQ a prerequisite for an absence of common sense? Or had the incentives and motivation become so distorted as to negate the exercise of the latter?

These large philosophical questions need to be posed and answered before a reconstruction of a durable new framework for the future can take place.

A world economy that was working quite steadily and growing regularly without wild swings in either direction should not have produced financial markets that behaved most of the time quite madly.

For this to have happened, the framework in which financial markets operated must have changed for the worse and developed deep flaws.

One obvious seismic change of course was the repeal of the Glass-Steagall Act in 1999 (as covered elsewhere in this text).

Up until 1999, we know that the financial sector of the economy in the US accounted for about 18% of the annual corporate profits. But by 2007 it had soared to a whopping 40%, after Glass-Steagall had been repealed.

Something drastically wrong had happened here to enable a small part of the capitalist system – the financial sector – to grab for itself such a disproportionate share of the overall wealth produced.

This had also distorted the national salary structure. Up until 1998 top bankers typically earned similar remuneration packages to top captains of industry. But by 2007 the bankers' remuneration had more than doubled compared to the rest of industry. There is nothing in economic history to suggest that bankers are more valuable to the economic system than captains of industry. Most would actually claim the opposite.

There are obviously other issues that have to be addressed, such as whether the new raft of derivative products created in this decade add at all to overall economic outcome, or actually pose a greater risk of undermining it.

Banking reform is now a supranational matter, being pored over by as many as 300 think tanks and bodies. Let us hope that an insightful pronouncement of President Truman does happen:

> Men make history, not the other way round. Progress occurs when courageous, skilful leaders seize the opportunity to change things for the better.

It will require courage as the banking lobby has a lot to lose, and will fight to maintain a system that implicitly means 'heads', they can win; and 'tails', when they lose, the rest of society picks up their bill.

Another aspect of this extraordinary decade has shown very conclusively how herd-like behaviour destroys wealth. Wild financial fluctuations are in nobody's interest, and, more often than not, are a sign of troubles ahead. These fluctuations, if left unchecked, interrupt economic progress and upset economic stability, thus damaging overall performance. It seems that regulators should devote more of their energies to supervision of, and mitigation, where possible, against these. But clearly it has to be an internationally coordinated effort.

One other issue, perhaps the most important of all, sticks out from this decade: It is the 'constant' that high price earnings, whether in an individual stock, or an entire market or sector, were a danger signal for potential losses ahead. There was no way of judging how high each Icarus would fly, only the certainty that if you overstayed, like him, you were burned. This is likely to be so in the future too, and a sharp warning to all long-term investors that high price earnings at some point get savagely brought down to earth.

March 2012 will be the twentieth anniversary of the death of one of the greatest political thinkers of the twentieth century, Professor Friedrich Hayek. In *The Road to Serfdom* of 1944 and *The Sensory Order* (published in 1952), he exposed the contradictions of totalitarian and socialist economic systems. Essentially, he explained philosophically that they were trying to do something that could not be done in the first place: this was based on the self evident proposition that a single human mind cannot comprehend something more complex than itself:

The proposition that we shall attempt to establish is that any apparatus of classification must possess a structure of a higher degree of complexity than is possessed by the objects that it classifies. Therefore the capacity of any explaining agent must be limited to objects with a structure possessing a degree of complexity lower than its own.

So a human mind, or a group of them for that matter, cannot act as 'an explaining agent' for a national economy, which represents the interaction of millions of minds.

This was his chief argument for preferring the rule of the market to the rule of government. This also, in investment knowledge terms, attracts me to 'charts' as a valuable backup or possibly filter to use when assessing research recommendations or market behaviour predictions.

By definition research recommendations are the actions of a single mind or a few minds trying to understand something usually much more complex than themselves. A chart tends to reflect the decisions of millions of minds at any given moment, and rather like 'the average of the guesses is better than the individual guesses in counting the number of jelly beans in a bottle' (what you learn at Harvard Business School!), charts can sometimes be a better guide to what is really happening, and sometimes a better pointer to what is going to happen, than the 'informed' research. But they are not easy to interpret.

Also, philosophically, I believe that Hayek's argument (that a human mind, or group thereof, cannot act as 'an explaining agent' for a national economy) points to the superiority of trying to seek market solutions rather than legislative ones to problems that arise. A good example of this is actually the dramatic improvement in the investment management industry since the bad days of the benchmark-tracking, index-hugging idiocies of the 1998–2003 period.

The free market voted with its feet, and the money moved to those fund managers who genuinely offered independent bespoke investment ideas. This led initially to a boom in hedge funds. These were eventually spoiled by too much money, sucking in poor or dubious operators. But those have largely been swept away now, leaving the best as survivors. I would say that, in spite of the FSA's counter-productive, benchmark-encouraging interference, the overall quality of funds now available to investors has never been better. The future is bright for the UK investment management industry.

In spite of the wild gyrations of this decade and no overall rise in the indices of the major western markets, it has nevertheless been possible to make money in equities provided one observed the basic principles of sound finance. These principles in general diminished the impetus to become sidetracked into fashions, fads and bubbles. Will-power has been required to resist being panicked into making silly sales of sound assets at rock-bottom prices during periodic stock market set-backs, or retaining assets that become patently overvalued and it has got to be said that never has a decade tested investors' will-power more frequently and sternly than this one.

Since politicians got their hands on the printing presses, after the demise of the gold standard, it has been difficult to believe a serious case can ever be made for bonds as a long-term asset class, especially for taxpayers where the accrual of value comes from the dividend only, and is thus drastically diminished by taxation.

A prudential cash or bond reserve is a standard element of sound financial management, whether for an individual or a business, as none of us possesses the foresight to know when the next economic downturn will happen, and nobody has yet eliminated the trade cycle or its random timing. But real assets, whether equity investments and/or property, must constitute the only serious long-term repository for savings and accumulated wealth.

Finally, I would like to make a plea for the inconsiderate conduct of many senior managers concerning long working hours for junior employees. In a very well argued book, *Management and Machiavelli,* by Antony Jay, the author, writes:

More and more of us have come to depend directly or indirectly on the patronage of vast organizations for our livelihoods, and on their behaviour for our quality of life.

Particularly in the City too many younger employees, especially in investment banking and legal firms, have their quality of life thoughtlessly blighted by ridiculously long working hours.

Any university tutor will tell you that the human mind is not capable of more than four hours of creative thought in any 24-hour period. The long hours are just stupid, and probably counter-productive in terms of useful output anyway. They are needlessly destructive of any hope of a reasonable social or family life. This is a consequence of industries whose leaders have lost all sense of proportion and consideration for the purpose of life, in a blind and reckless pursuit of the extra shekel.

The management argument – it was done to us so why should they not endure it! – reminds one of a reflection of that great French philosopher and political thinker, Montesquieu, some 200 years ago: 'The fixity of habit is in exact proportion to its absurdity.' These managers would also do well to remember what that legendary investor, Peter Lynch, said: 'You remind yourself that nobody on his deathbed said: "I wish I had spent more time in the office."'